Teaching Online for Kindergarten and Primary Teachers

This practical guide to online teaching is for kindergarten teachers and primary or elementary teachers. It is based on research, teacher interviews, and the author's real-world experience working in online education, as both a teacher and a trainer.

Macur signposts relevant research and gives examples of key themes, tools, and ideas that can be applied in everyday teaching. These include a range of fundamental aspects of the online environment, with chapters covering online platforms, classroom management, student engagement, and feedback. It offers tried-and-tested exercises, takeaways, and reflective questions to give the reader numerous moments to consider how they will use, adapt, and develop these tools and integrate them into their own teaching practice.

Teaching Online for Kindergarten and Primary Teachers is a clear, informative, and pragmatic book for all educators and students to deepen their knowledge and prepare them for teaching online and delivering effective online education like a professional.

Gregory Michael Adam Macur is an elementary teacher, school leader, teacher trainer, and published educational researcher. As a University of Sunderland faculty member, he supports their PGCE program, supporting teacher trainees through contributing lectures, advice, guidance, and lesson observation/feedback.

Gregory Macur has written a must-read primer for kindergarten and primary school teachers who are or planning to teach in an online setting.
Dr. Evrim Erbilgin, Emirates College for Advanced Education & Editor at the Journal of Inquiry Based Activities, UAE

What Gregory has provided here is an informed, informative, critically-astute, and practical guide for teachers in online settings. He has embraced the trials and tribulations resulting from the pandemic, emerged at the practical forefront of his field, and has duly determined to support his colleagues with their online teaching.
Ian Elliott, University of Sunderland Board of Governors, PGCE Programme Leader, and Senior Fellow HEA

Gregory gives us all confidence to face our online lessons with competence. Writing about what's important to you is no mean feat. A valuable resource to the teaching toolkit.
André Double, Head of Primary at Invictus School Shenzhen

The book, uniquely, serves in providing straight-forward contextual examples of how to navigate the online teaching environment. It is precise, invaluable information for professionals and those seeking development.
Steven Stewart. PGCE, B.Sc, M.Sc, Nord Anglia teaching professional

Teaching Online for Kindergarten and Primary Teachers

Getting Ready for Your Next Online Class

Gregory Michael Adam Macur

Routledge
Taylor & Francis Group
LONDON AND NEW YORK

Cover image: Getty images

First published 2023
by Routledge
4 Park Square, Milton Park, Abingdon, Oxon OX14 4RN

and by Routledge
605 Third Avenue, New York, NY 10158

Routledge is an imprint of the Taylor & Francis Group, an informa business

© 2023 Gregory Michael Adam Macur

The right of Gregory Michael Adam Macur to be identified as author of this work has been asserted in accordance with sections 77 and 78 of the Copyright, Designs and Patents Act 1988.

All rights reserved. No part of this book may be reprinted or reproduced or utilised in any form or by any electronic, mechanical, or other means, now known or hereafter invented, including photocopying and recording, or in any information storage or retrieval system, without permission in writing from the publishers.

Trademark notice: Product or corporate names may be trademarks or registered trademarks, and are used only for identification and explanation without intent to infringe.

British Library Cataloguing-in-Publication Data
A catalogue record for this book is available from the British Library

Library of Congress Cataloging-in-Publication Data
Names: Macur, Gregory Michael Adam, author.
Title: Teaching online for kindergarten and primary teachers : getting ready for your next online class / Gregory Michael Adam Macur.
Description: Abingdon, Oxon ; New York, NY : Routledge, 2023. | Includes bibliographical references and index.
Identifiers: LCCN 2022013191 (print) | LCCN 2022013192 (ebook) | ISBN 9781032168562 (hardback) | ISBN 9781032168548 (paperback) | ISBN 9781003250630 (ebook)
Subjects: LCSH: Kindergarten—Computer-assisted instruction. | Education, Primary—Computer-assisted instruction. | Web-based instruction. | Internet in education.
Classification: LCC LB1169 .M24 2023 (print) | LCC LB1169 (ebook) | DDC 371.33/44678—dc23/eng/20220521
LC record available at https://lccn.loc.gov/2022013191
LC ebook record available at https://lccn.loc.gov/2022013192

ISBN: 978-1-032-16856-2 (hbk)
ISBN: 978-1-032-16854-8 (pbk)
ISBN: 978-1-003-25063-0 (ebk)

DOI: 10.4324/9781003250630

Typeset in Optima
by Apex CoVantage, LLC

This book is dedicated to my mother, Iwona Macur, and grandmother, Stephania Macur. Thank you for giving so much to raise me and Sean.

Contents

List of tables	xii
Preface	xiii
Before you read this book, ask yourself these questions	xiii
A note from the author	xiv
Why you should read this book	xv
Why I wrote this book	xv
Disclaimer	xvi
1 Introduction	**1**
Aims of the chapter	1
Introduction	2
What is the structure of this book and how does it benefit you?	3
What is online education?	5
Why should you know about online education?	5
Conclusion	6
Key takeaways	7
2 Platforms you can use	**8**
Aims of the chapter	8
Done right vs. done wrong	9
Introduction	11
What are the functions to look out for in an online platform?	12
What are the functions to look out for in an online platform?	14
Platforms you could use	16
Conclusion	19
Key takeaways	20

Contents

3	**Classroom management online**	**23**
	Aims of the chapter	23
	Done right vs. done wrong	24
	Introduction	26
	What are the benefits of classroom management?	27
	Why do students misbehave?	28
	Rules in the online classroom	31
	Positive classroom management	34
	Conclusion	37
	Key takeaways	37
4	**Online student engagement**	**41**
	Aims of the chapter	41
	Done right vs. done wrong	42
	Introduction	44
	What are the benefits of student engagement?	45
	How to motivate students intrinsically vs. extrinsically	47
	What are different methods of applying reward systems?	50
	Interaction patterns and engagement	52
	Context, meaningful learning, and gamification?	55
	Conclusion	57
	Key takeaways	57
5	**Body language and instructions in the online classroom**	**61**
	Aims of the chapter	61
	Done right vs. done wrong	62
	Introduction	64
	How gestures, cues, and body language help in an online lesson	65
	How to use correct posture and why it is both healthy and helpful	67
	How to give instructions and tricks to support this in an online class	69
	Methods of modelling and demonstrating tasks online	71
	Conclusion	73
	Key takeaways	74

Contents

6	**Working with parents online**	**77**
	Aims of the chapter	77
	Done right vs. done wrong	78
	Introduction	80
	The benefits that can be reaped from parent communication, interaction, and involvement	82
	Potential barriers/problems and overcoming them	83
	Effective ways to communicate with parents	85
	Things parents should and shouldn't help with	87
	Conclusion	88
	Key takeaways	89
7	**Big classes, small classes, and 1-to-1**	**92**
	Aims of the chapter	92
	Done right vs. done wrong	93
	Introduction	95
	How to overcome the challenges of teaching big classes	96
	How to overcome the challenges of teaching small classes	97
	How to overcome the challenges of teaching 1-to-1	98
	Conclusion	99
	Key takeaways	100
8	**Error correction and feedback online**	**103**
	Aims of the chapter	103
	Done right vs. done wrong	104
	Introduction	106
	What are some of the key types of student errors?	107
	What are some of the causes of errors?	108
	When and why timing of error correction is important	109
	Methods of error correction	110
	How to use positive error correction	111
	What ways can you give feedback?	112
	Conclusion	113
	Key takeaways	114

Contents

9	**Assessment – assessing students online**	**117**
	Aims of the chapter	117
	Done right vs. done wrong	118
	Introduction	120
	Online assessment's benefits and challenges	121
	What is diagnostic assessment?	123
	What is assessment for learning (AFL)?	124
	What is assessment of learning (AOL)?	125
	What is assessment as learning (AAL)?	127
	Conclusion	128
	Key takeaways	129
10	**Online student welfare and wellbeing**	**132**
	Aims of the chapter	132
	Done right vs. done wrong	133
	Introduction	134
	Eye safety during online lessons	135
	The importance of movement	137
	Consideration of lesson lengths	138
	Safeguarding	138
	Conclusion	140
	Key takeaways	141
11	**Activities – online teaching and learning strategies**	**144**
	Aims of the chapter	145
	Done right vs. done wrong	145
	Introduction	147
	Setting context	148
	Warm-up activities	152
	Teacher-fronted approach	155
	Student-centred activities	158
	Project-based learning	162
	Inquiry-based learning	165
	Routines	167
	Differentiation	170
	Flipped learning	173

Blended learning	175
Reflection and wrap-up	176
Conclusion	177
Key takeaways	178

12 Things your students should have ready for classes — 182
Great things students can have ready for online classes	182
Things you do not want students to have around them during online classes	183
How to inform parents of these?	184

13 What to take from this book — 186
Do this, do that!	186
Now you have read this book, ask yourself these questions again – this time, answer them	187
So . . . what do I take?	188

Final note — 189
To the reader	189
To the publisher	189
To my mentors	190
To the people who put up with me disappearing to finish this	190

Index — 191

Tables

2.1	Matching teacher needs with platform functions	17
3.1	Causes of misbehaviour, solutions to this, and how this may look in a real online classroom	29
3.2	Examples of positive and negative rules	32
5.1	How body language, gestures, and cues can solve common problems in the online classroom	65
5.2	Methods of modelling and demonstrating in the online classroom	72
6.1	Potential barriers and problems while working with parents – and how to overcome them	84
8.1	An example of sandwiched feedback	113
9.1	The benefits and challenges of online assessments	121
12.1	Example online learning space guidelines	185

Preface

Before you read this book, ask yourself these questions

1 What opportunities are there for you to enhance your practice through the use of platforms? What variety of ways can these platforms support you? Can you reduce your marking workload? Can you provide a more student-centred learning environment through the use of these technologies?
2 What is classroom management? How can classroom management be utilised in an online setting? Can this be positive? What about engaging the students? What options are there for bringing these two concepts to life?
3 How can body language and instructions support your online lessons? What about posture and a proper learning environment set up?
4 What role do parents play in online learning? How can they support you? What are they worried about? How can you alleviate this worry?
5 How will you approach the teaching of different class sizes online? What challenges and opportunities will this present?
6 How will you correct students' errors online? How will you feed back to your students? How can students' errors provide feedback to you as a teacher?
7 What about assessment? What types of assessment are there? How can you use these in your online practice? How can assessments inform you about the students, curriculum, and yourself?
8 Student welfare is key in online learning. What are some of the core ways to support student welfare when teaching online? How can you

integrate these into your practice? Where can you find out information about safeguarding?
9 What kind of activities can you use when teaching online? How will you adapt them to suit your students and lessons?
10 What should students have ready for class? What do you not want them to have? How will you communicate this to parents?

These are the questions that you will find answers to in this book. As you read the book, reflect on these questions and yourself as an online teacher. Underline and highlight key points as you read; this will come in handy during the reflection moment in Chapter 13, "What to Take From This Book." In that chapter, we revisit these questions, giving you an opportunity to reflect on them with the new knowledge, tools, and skills that you have acquired.

A note from the author

As educators, we find ourselves constantly surrounded by learning and development. It is the world in which we have chosen to exist, live, and thrive. We hold expectations on our students of growth, change, development, critical thought, and openness to ideas. However, too often, we do not live by our own expectations and advice. We limit our own growth by clinging too desperately to what we have learnt or what we are learning. For that reason, the following short paragraph is included:

The ideas in this book are not the only ones in the world – they are also not the "perfect" ideas for you; look at each page and take value in what stands out to you as applicable and pragmatic for you as a teacher. Build on the ideas that you find; build on the themes and develop your own practice. You will know your teaching practice, students, context, environment, and educational objectives far better than I ever will. This being the case, act intuitively, read further research yourself, criticise the ideas I put forward and the ones you find in your research, navigate your own pathway through this educational world, and build a truly research-, evidence-, and experience-based teaching practice. The best thing you can do, then, is to share all of your knowledge with the people around you, listening carefully to their ideas and feedback.

If we ever stop changing and growing, because we feel as though we have mastered our environment, entropy will change the environment and swallow us up. So, keep learning.

Why you should read this book

Covid-19 changed the world; it opened our eyes to the possibility and likelihood of viruses closing schools and public areas. As a result, we now need teachers who are online education competent. This book equips you with knowledge of the research, tools, tips, and tricks that allow you to navigate this new domain of education as a professional.

All of the ideas put forward in the book are based on a combination of related research; interviews with over 100 professional teachers and trainers; surveys spanning 40 countries regarding teacher perspectives of problem areas when teaching online; and this author's own experience both teaching online and training teachers within this domain. This means that the strategies presented are tried and tested.

This book is laid out in a manner that allows you as a reader to skip to any chapter you feel is relevant and read it, understand it, and take value from it.

Within the chapters, a consistent structure is followed. This structure enables you to pick out key parts of the chapter that are important to you and to skip over parts with which you are perhaps already familiar. That being said, there are always gems lurking in the depths; as such, I recommend reading it in its entirety.

Finally, this book is written in a digestible and accessible manner. It is written with stories and examples embedded within it. It is also written in a way that allows anyone to access the content, whether you are an experienced teacher with years of online practice, a newly qualified teacher looking to begin building your toolkit, or, an aspiring teacher getting ready for your new career.

Why I wrote this book

Having taught online with various schools over the last few years (prior to Covid), I found myself to be a big fan of online education and yet, simultaneously, its biggest critic. I enjoyed the freedom it gave us as teachers, but I missed all of the tools we have in a traditional classroom. I soldiered on, eyes wide open for how to recapture key educational approaches like group work and project-based learning. Over the years, I found myself gradually coming across research that gave me ideas of how to improve my online practice. I also found that the technology was improving nicely.

When Covid-19 happened, my school group at the time, which had well over 150 teachers in the region in which I was the mentor, needed to start delivering classes online. The only problem was, none of the teachers had taught online before, and we did not have an online curriculum. So, I started working with the research and development team to put together an online curriculum, and then I created a training program for the teachers. As we ran through the training program, I saw the impact this had on the teachers' practice. I got a great deal of satisfaction from seeing the practical improvements teachers were experiencing, and the positive feedback also spurred me on.

Seeing the new technologies that have become available since then, and having gained a greater depth of understanding and online education know-how, I started to think about methods through which I could continue to help teachers develop their online practice. As a writer, doing research, writing articles, and producing this book were the logical next steps.

I wanted to create a practical, pragmatic book, based on experience, research, and the opinions of hundreds of teachers, that could be easily digested and utilised quickly by all teachers. A book written by a teacher, for all teachers.

Disclaimer

As the author of this book, I have no affiliation to any of the platforms referred to, nor do I recommend you use them or not use them. They are simply used as examples of what is available. It is up to you as a reader to research the options available, looking out for the functions that stand out to you as the most pragmatic and essential. All of the ideas conveyed in this book are formulated to the best of my ability at present, based on both the prominent educational research of past and present and my own experience.

# Introduction

My first ever online lesson was a catastrophe. Everything that you would want to avoid, happened. Everything that you want to see in a good lesson was absent. It made me think that teaching online was impossible. This is not the case; my trainer ran through some simple tips and tricks with me, and my catastrophic lesson turned into an okay one (which is a pretty good trajectory if you ask me!). The reason I begin with this story is because if you are currently teaching online, or are about to, there is no need to think that the problems you will face (and you will face them) are insurmountable. If I can become a great online teacher and trainer, anybody can! This section really just sets the scene, but the whole book will be your own toolkit, to adapt and apply as you see fit.

This chapter provides an introduction to online education and the structure of this book. How you might go about reading this book is briefly touched on, too. There are some key definitions and justifications for the manner and style in which the book is written.

Aims of the chapter

> *By the end of this chapter, you will know:*
>
> - *What is the structure of this book?*
> - *How does the structure benefit you?*
> - *What is online education?*
> - *Why should you know about online education?*

DOI: 10.4324/9781003250630-1

Introduction

In recent years, online education has become a fundamental cornerstone of any teacher's pedagogy (Allen & Seaman, 2013). This is partly due to technological developments and partly due to increased access to the internet globally, but mostly, it is down to the Covid-19 situation that swallowed up the world (De' R, 2020). Covid-19 has acted as a fundamental driver of this domain of education since 2019. According to UNESCO, the number of students worldwide that have had their normal school life impacted is record-breaking (UNESCO, 2020). This being the case, now is the time to update our pedagogy and online teaching toolkit. In doing this, we can improve the standards of online education and meet our learners' needs in this new context.

There are many negative outcomes that this situation created; however, one clear, positive outcome, educationally speaking, is the development and growth of education in an online setting (De' R, 2020). Now, it is important to note that I am not saying we should be abandoning the traditional classroom; the benefits of interacting in a more physical setting as opposed to a digital one are plentiful (Arias et al., 2018). What I am saying, though, is that vast improvements to the pedagogy and toolkit of online education is, on all counts, a great thing. The reason I say this is simple; the global manner in which education can be spread through the online setting means that teachers and students from all around the world can connect. Theoretically, this makes education more accessible, especially as computers and internet usage have become more widespread, even in the poorest of countries (World Bank, 2020).

Increased access to online education and pressure on schools to provide education online have facilitated the technology that was previously in place. As a result, there are many new methods we can use to engage our students in the online setting. The manner by which education can be distributed is already being used in fantastic ways. Gavin McCormack, an educational leader, spent the better part of 2021 reading children's books aloud online. He did this every evening so that children around the world could have access to these stories (thousands of children tuned in). This has had an incredible impact in areas of the world where English as an additional language (EAL) learners have been able to engage with English children's storybooks on a daily basis.

What is the structure of this book and how does it benefit you?

This book is written in a structured, clear, and informative manner. The chapters are laid out in a cumulative manner, progressing through platforms you can use; classroom management; student engagement; body language and instructions; working with parents online; big classes, small classes, and 1-to-1; error correction and feedback; assessment; student welfare; activities (online teaching and learning strategies); things your students should have ready; and what to take from this book. Although these chapters stack on top of each other very well, they are written in a way such that when read alone, or in any order, they are understandable and informative.

The major benefit of this approach, for you as a reader, busy teacher, educator, etc., is simple: if you are looking for some key information, or to brush up on two or three of the topics covered, you can jump right into them without having to start the book at the beginning, saving you valuable time. It also means that if there are some chapters you feel well informed about and comfortable with already and have no desire to read, you can skip them. I would advise at least skimming over the ones you feel confident in, however, as in the past, I have missed out on great nuggets of information when doing this.

Each chapter also follows a very logical progression internally. Beneath the chapter title, there is a paragraph relating to a moment I have encountered as a teacher, followed by a concise paragraph that states what the chapter is about.

Following this is a bulleted list of the aims of the chapter, which shows you as a reader what you can expect to be absorbing while you read. There is additional information in the chapter beyond these key learning points, and this information is also useful to absorb; however, the list gives you an idea of what is fundamentally important.

After this comes a done right vs. done wrong section, which presents two scenarios, one where some of the skills and tools we learned about in the chapter are used well, causing a positive learning environment and experience; and one where the skills and tools are poorly applied or totally missing, causing a chaotic, unproductive, and unenjoyable learning environment for both learner and teacher. Think of these scenarios as essential context setters to make it all the more real, tangible, pragmatic, and

Introduction

purposeful for you as a teacher. All scenarios are based on real classrooms and real circumstances I have observed when assessing teachers (some are from my own practice). These scenarios really emphasise why the tools you can acquire from reading this book are beneficial and how they can impact your classroom. They are written in engaging, story-like ways; this is purposeful, intended to enhance the reading experience for you.

The next section is the introduction, which will define the concept/topic the chapter focuses on and/or review some of the prominent research both past and present. There are some additional points about the main premise and the structure of ideas within the chapter. This ensures you have that groundwork in place before jumping into the research and practice.

Next comes research and practical application – something all teachers care about, and the section that some may skip to. Here, we look at the relevant tools available for you to use to get your classroom closer to the "optimal" scenario we read at the start of the chapter. I use the word "optimal" in quotations because there are many ways a classroom can manifest a healthy learning environment. So, don't think that this section is a rubric for teachers' online practice in order to make them identical practice producing robots; I advocate against teachers doing this to students in an article for *Times Educational Supplement* titled: "We Can't Let Rubrics Turn Us Into Robo-Teachers." It is actually a tools list for you to adapt, take from, and apply in your own practice, in your own way, with your own students. When you find better ways of doing things, and you will, that is great; share your tools on social media and through word-of-mouth with your co-teachers. We are all in this together, and sharing our experience is the best way for us all to grow and improve.

As with all good chapters, there is a brief conclusion; this is concise and clear, a wrapping up of the definitions, research, and practice that was covered. This also acts somewhat as a recap and gives you some ideas about moving forward. This section is more like the end of a lesson than a deep analysis, as it recaps and consolidates.

Finally, there is a key takeaways box. This is a bulleted list of the main concepts, tools, and ideas that you should have taken from the chapter. While reading this, it is a good idea to highlight the key points that you found to be useful and to write down how you plan to implement them in your own practice. This list does not contain all of the content from the chapter, so feel free to find your own key learning points as you move through the book.

What is online education?

My first mentor described education to me as "all about learning, growth and development, not getting kids to think what we want them to. It is more about getting kids to be able to think more effectively. When we work as teachers, we need to remember that." While this is a good start, let's look a little deeper.

For the purpose of coming to a well-considered definition of online education, these two words will be first defined separately in simple and straight-forward ways and then knitted back together, enriched, and enhanced, with consideration of the words as a whole.

"Online" is a term that is said to have first been used in relation to the railroads and the transportation of coal, with "online" being "on the line" and "offline" being "off the line." Now, this term is used when we talk about being connected to the internet, something found on the internet, being linked up to a network, system, or set of areas through the use of technology, and being up and running (Merriam Webster, n.d.).

Education is the processes, systems, and instructions that revolve around the learning, growth, and development of individuals and groups. Typically, this is associated with schools, universities, and courses of instruction that aim towards the betterment of all relevant stakeholders; however, education can be seen in a more general sense and considered as a way of attending to things/opening up doorways (Ingold, 2017). Education happens in schools, in homes, in parks, and in all of the places we find ourselves.

Knitting these two terms together brings about a beautiful concept. Online education is the process by which individuals and groups grow, learn, and develop, in global and interconnected ways, through the medium of internet-based networks and schools, which are geared towards the improvement of all people, especially the students involved.

Why should you know about online education?

As a teacher, you will undoubtedly be hurled into the online teaching environment; this is almost guaranteed in the current educational environment. As such, you need to be prepared to contend with this new monster (scary though it may be). It is also important to know that simply doing what is prescribed in the traditional classroom setting does not work in the online setting. For example, in a large class in a traditional classroom, short, quick-fire pair chats work very well; however, in an online classroom, setting up break out rooms (see Chapter 2 on platforms) for brief pair chats is often not cost-effective with regard to timing. That being said, we can steal ideas from our traditional classroom pedagogy and then adapt, improve, and transform them to make them more appropriate for the online teaching environment.

As a kindergarten and primary teacher, it is important to keep your online pedagogy and know-how up to date. Having this toolkit readily available will improve your teaching practice, enhance your CV, boost your competence in job interviews, and give you a deeper sense of confidence when teaching online. Also, when applying for positions, you will certainly to be asked about how you approach online teaching practice.

The multiplicity of benefits that come alongside being well informed about a key aspect of your profession goes on and could be made into a book on its own. However, for the purpose of this concise introduction, this is enough.

Conclusion

Online education is a rapidly growing industry, fuelled by technological developments and shifts in the global environment such as the Covid-19 pandemic (De' R, 2020).

Online education is the coming together of learning, development, and growth being delivered through networks and internet-based schooling. As teachers, there are a multiplicity of benefits to be reaped from being well informed about this topic, such as improved teaching practice and a competitive advantage in interviews. This means that reading this book, and putting into practice the tools presented, is a good idea for any kindergarten/primary school teacher.

The best way to read this book is from start to finish; however, due to the stand-alone nature of each chapter, it is possible only to read the chapters you feel are relevant to you. This is also true with regard to individual sections within the chapters.

Key takeaways

- *Online education is all about learning, growth, and development through network/internet-based mediums.*
- *Knowing about online education provides benefits such as improved teaching practice and a competitive advantage in interviews.*
- *This book is structured cumulatively; however, each chapter can be read and understood on its own.*
- *Each chapter is broken down into the following segments: aims, scenarios, introduction, research and practice, conclusion, and key takeaways.*

Bibliography

Allen, I. E., & Seaman, J. (2013). *Changing course: Ten years of tracking online education in the United States*. Sloan Consortium.

Arias, J. J., Swinton, J., & Anderson, K. (2018). Online vs. face-to-face: A comparison of student outcomes with random assignment. *E-Journal of Business Education and Scholarship of Teaching*, 1–23.

De' R, P. N. (2020). Impact of digital surge during Covid-19 pandemic: A viewpoint on research and practice. *International Journal of Information Management, 55*, 102171.

Ingold, T. (2017). *Anthropology and/as education*. Routledge.

Merriam Webster. (n.d.). *Definition of online*. Retrieved September 7, 2021, from www.merriam-webster.com/dictionary/online

UNESCO. (2020). *COVID-19 educational disruption and response*. Retrieved September 14, 2021, from UNESCO: https://en.unesco.org/covid19/educationresponse/solutions

World Bank. (2020). *Individuals using the internet (% of population)*. The World Bank.

Platforms you can use

When I first tried to teach an online lesson, the platform I used was complicated and it felt like it would take me about three years to learn how to use it. This was the same story for my students. It went down every 5 minutes and did not have a chat box function, which meant that when microphones were not working, we all had to attempt sign language to communicate as we could not hear what the other person was saying. Since then, through reading the research, interviewing teachers, observing teachers, and teaching online myself, I have learnt what to look out for and will share it with you here.

This chapter gives you an idea of the different types of online platform that are available for you to consider, such as live video platforms or quiz platforms. Things to look for and things to avoid are listed. The conclusion of this chapter is that teachers should take some value from each of the platforms that are available, using them in the best combination for their position.

Aims of the chapter

By the end of this chapter, you will know:

- *What are online platforms?*
- *What are the functions to look out for in an online platform?*
- *What are the functions to avoid in an online platform?*
- *What are some examples of platforms you can use?*

Done right vs. done wrong

The following are two online classroom scenarios. Scenario A is an example of a classroom in which the teacher has not utilised the platforms available to them properly, causing difficulty, boredom, and additional work. Scenario B is an example of a classroom in which the teacher has considered and utilised the platforms that they could use, and the tools these platforms provide, creating an engaging lesson and a lower workload for the teacher after class has ended.

Scenario A

Eyes glazed over for all involved, the students and teacher get ready for class. The teacher starts the video call, and slowly students begin to answer. The ones who don't answer need to be re-called; there is no option for them to enter the session once the ring tone stops. This means that students often do not attend class. For those who do, the teacher begins lecturing; while there are some concept-checking questions asked in a plenary manner, the students mostly just listen to the teacher perpetually speak (or not). This is a process that many adults struggle to engage with, let alone kindergarten or primary students. In defence of the poor teacher, using a platform that only allows you to video call and nothing more does make it difficult to increase student participation.

The platform goes down – three times, to be specific. When the teacher finally gets it back up, half of the students do not return. Even 10 minutes of this is enough for them to know they don't want to continue.

Once the input has been completed, the students are set individual worksheet tasks; once complete, they must take a photograph of it and submit to the teacher via email. This way the teacher can mark them by either using an image editor like Paint or printing them out, marking them by hand, and then emailing them back (this is a real process I have seen people do, and yes, it is as time-consuming and bureaucratic as it sounds).

After the individual work is completed, the teacher asks a few plenary questions to assess whether the students have learnt the main concepts: students touch their heads for yes and touch their nose for no to answer these. This is not a bad way to assess; it does work better if the students close their eyes, though, as otherwise they may simply copy their peers.

Platforms you can use

Homework is set; the students need to answer ten multiple choice questions and write a short paragraph about the things they learnt in the lesson. The class is over, and a breath of relief is sighed by all. Next comes 30 pieces of work to mark; the teacher puts their head in their hands and thinks: "Surely there is a better way to do this . . ."

Scenario B

The teacher heads over to their computer. Lesson: prepped! Coffee: drunk! Homework marking done? – please . . . it marked itself!

The students rush over to their computers, eager to see their friends and work on group projects.

The teacher opens up the interactive platform. Some students are already in the class; as long as they have the invitation code, they can show up – no need to bombard them with calls. This means that late students can still join once the class has started (although the teacher works with the parents to avoid student lateness).

The teacher starts to use the screen share function (this shares the teacher's screen with the students) and opens up a game of boggle (a game where students get some letters and need to make as many words as possible). The students, engaged, get on with this while waiting for the class start time (the student with the most words gets a message sent to their parents telling them about this).

The class begins. Using the screen share function, the teacher plays the students a short video introducing the topic; before playing the video, the teacher asks them to write down what they think the topic is. When the video is finished, the teacher opens up the draw/write function (this allows the students to draw/write on the teacher's shared screen); the students need to write down what they think the topic is. Most get it – the rainforest.

Next, the students are put into break out rooms in groups of four (these allow you to put groups of students into separate online rooms to work together). They are going to research the reasons rainforests are important and put together a short presentation explaining this.

The teacher moves between the break out groups, supporting students where necessary and providing research support links, e.g. Thinglink (see the platforms section), for students who need it.

The presentations are delivered and are a great success. The multiple-choice homework for the class is set through a self-grading quiz application and the reflection on learning is set as a voice note to be sent through the class chat group. The teacher thinks back to when they used to teach online through just a video call and breathes a sigh of relief.

> *When it comes to the platforms you use for your online classes, practical tools are everything. Scenario B shows just how much more engaging lessons can be and how much of the workload can be taken off if you utilise even some of the tools available to online teachers and students. Now, let's look at what we mean by platforms in a bit more detail; then, we will see what the research tells us and how we can improve our online practice as a result of it.*

Introduction

When we say "online platform," what we mean is a website, program, or application that can be used to enhance your online teaching practice. Some are absolutely essential, like the application you use to video call with your students. Others are non-essential extras to make your life easier, like a quiz website that has a self-marking function or, my personal favourite, ones to make the lessons more engaging for the students, like add-ons that can put cartoon ears on you while you teach or turn you into an animal. In a perfect world, all of these would be embedded in one supreme platform, but currently, they are not, so you need to find out what kinds of things to look out for, what things to avoid, and examples of platforms that you could use.

A good way to think of online platforms and their functions is in comparison to the tools you have in the classroom. Sometimes, you pull out the markers, hand-held boards, and rubbers (think draw function), sometimes you shuffle the kids into groups of four and rearrange the tables (think break out rooms), and, almost always, you use a PowerPoint, Smart Board, or video resources (think screen-share function).

Online platforms can even go beyond the tools we have in the classroom; they have a wide range of functions to support teachers. We are going to introduce and discuss the range of said functions and the creative ways these can be used. However, what we cover is only a fraction of the creative ways to apply these. As you read, be mindful of other methods of utilising platforms and functions to make your life easier and lessons more engaging for the students.

The next section looks at some of the research that links to this topic and the practical application and tools available to you as a teacher. While you read this section, think about the different ways in which you can adapt these tools to suit your own teaching methodology.

What are the functions to look out for in an online platform?

In this section, we will refer to platforms as tools/platforms and to the things the platform can do as functions; sometimes the word tools may be used, too. We will give some platform options to look out for, based on educational research, after we have discussed the functions. It should be noted, we are not recommending platforms but simply stating some options; it is up to you to try some of them out and find the ones that work well for your school and/or practice.

The plethora of platforms to choose from is extensive, and their functions even more so. So, what should you be looking out for? Huang et al. (2020) argued that convenience for teachers is a key component that should be considered. The tool itself should help teachers do a few things, including:

- Helping teachers create resources easily.
- Helping teachers manage resources easily.
- Publishing notifications to students.
- Managing and organising students.
- Allowing students to obtain resources.
- Having functions whereby students can participate in learning activities simply.
- Providing quick and easy methods of communication.
- Giving feedback to parents.
- Tracking students' progress and performance.

(Huang et al., 2020)

For anybody who has ever worked or trained as a teacher, these key points ring true and we understand their importance. We understand their importance because we have always tried to set up our own classroom and teaching practice in a manner that also ticks these boxes. Finding an online platform with these functions will make your life much easier and will support your students' learning experience. We will explore what kind of functions will do this and some of the applications that may provide these functions. Remember, the list is not a "use this app" list; it is just a list. Go and do your research and find applications, platforms, and websites that work for you, your students, and your school.

Enhancing online learning

Research by Hrastinski (2009) advocated that to enhance online teaching and learning, we need to enhance participation on the learner side. This reminded me of a kindergarten lesson that I observed. We were using an interactive platform (one where students can draw/write/move things on the screen). The teacher had set up a lesson where students all got a chance to take advantage of these interactive options; as a result, the student participation rates were high, and this resulted in fewer behavioural problems, more motivated students, and a much more relaxed teacher. When teaching younger students, we cannot expect them to sit and listen to a lecture the same way we do with university students; it simply does not work. As such, look out for an online platform with interactive elements and break out room functions.

Increasing interaction is a great way to enhance and improve enthusiasm for learning and concentration (Chen et al., 2020). There are many ways to increase interaction during online learning, and we will look at them a little more deeply in our chapter on student engagement. However, with regard to the platform that you use, it is a good idea to find ones that have functions that actually allow students to interact, such as break out room functions and live chat boxes.

David and Glore (2010) showed that having visual elements embedded within the lesson impacted and improved participation and user interaction. We have all seen this in our lessons; there is a reason a PPT or smart presentation uses images and not large swaths of text. Most live video streaming platforms will allow you to at least screen share, so you can deliver your lesson as you would in a physical classroom. If you choose a platform with only this additional function, it is worth setting activities that get the students to engage (such as mini teacher), or at least use plenty of plenary questions to get whole class responses.

What are the functions to look out for in an online platform?

There are many opinions about what makes an online educational platform, website, or application subpar. I have my own pet hates, which are all covered by what the research indicates (unreliable platforms!). Let's look at what the research says.

Asarbakhsh and Sandars (2013) put forward that technology failure, system break downs, disrupted/failed video connection, and unusable functions led to negative impacts on user satisfaction. This makes sense to us all; nobody likes it when they are trying to watch a show, load an email, or download a document, and it doesn't work. The frustration it causes is often also more exaggerated than the problem it causes. Seeing this happen during lessons to teachers and students is not a pretty sight. This idea is backed up by a 2020 study that showed that the most negatively impacting factor for students while learning online was "network congestion." This was voted for over twice as many times as "insufficient learning resources" (Chen et al., 2020), which is surprising considering the learning resources are what they signed up for. So, make sure you do your research on the reliability of your platform. Sometimes it is better to go with what is very well known and used, as opposed to what is brand new and very innovative but potentially less tried and tested.

Research by Chen et al. (2020) brought to light three other key factors that negatively impacted the online learning experience:

- The design of the platform should be simple and user friendly, and offer useful functions such as "dark mode" so that, in the evening, students' eyes can be better protected. So, avoid platforms with complicated designs and difficult to use functions.

It is worth noting that almost all laptops, phones, and computers have a night light option embedded within them now. Simply telling your students to put this on will do the same thing. The key thing to remember here is that the simple and user-friendly design is extremely important, as are simple, practical extra functions. The last thing you want is to spend the first ten lessons teaching the students how to use the platform.

- Platforms should be accessible to different types of electrical devices: phones, tablets, iPads, computers and laptops, etc. The platform should also support a screen rotation function, so the user can have the device turned in the manner in which they feel most comfortable. So, avoid platforms that are restricted to certain devices and app stores.

This kind of information can be easily found by doing a simple internet search of the platform and its functions/availability to devices. Another possible way to figure this out is to go onto their website and contact their customer support (no customer support? Bad sign!).

- Customer services are essential. When using an online platform, online customer service should always be available to support users with problems and reduce/prevent the loss and wastage of learning time. So, avoid platforms with no support.

This links back to an earlier section where we mentioned that aiming for tried-and-tested platforms and companies may be a better option than moving towards brand new and innovative. This is absolutely not always the case, but especially for new online teachers, having additional barriers and problems to potentially face, is not a good idea (Chen et al., 2020).

Impacting online learning satisfaction

Roca et al. (2006) analysed online learning satisfaction and came to find that the user's satisfaction was impacted in a number of ways; these correspond with Chen et al. (2020) and Asarbakhsh and Sandars (2013). The four main determinants were:

- Perceived usefulness and quality of the course.
- The degree of expected achievement.

These first two determinants, while not exactly directly related to the platform, are important to consider. As such, the platform you use should be able to offer some support. For example, if you can screen share and play a video of students using what you have taught in their real lives, it would make the course seem more purposeful. And if you have an option to share images, you could send out graphic images that demonstrate previous student pass rates.

- The quality of the platform.

This is on you; do your research, read reviews, try the platform out, and make sure it is user friendly for both you and your students. Most of the platforms out there can either be used freely or will give you a short trial. If not, subscribe to it at your own risk. Finally, remember, sometimes too many functions is actually a bad thing; you don't want your students to be overwhelmed.

- The website service.

This links back to Chen et al. (2020) again; the website should be well maintained and have support staff available 24/7 in case there are platform problems and you need to get a function fixed to get on with your lesson.

The next section will briefly describe 6/7 platforms, apps, and websites that can be used. There are many other options out there, and Google is a wonderful tool for finding them. Do not limit yourself to the options listed here. Think more about what functions the research indicates they need and then apply that level of requirement to the platforms that you decide upon for your own practice.

Platforms you could use

There are many platforms, apps, and websites out there for you. We are going to look at 6/7 that I have used/seen teachers use successfully and that are reflected thoroughly in the research. I will give some very simple suggestions as to how/why these might be used and then link this back to the research as to which platform could tick which boxes. This section will not tell you explicitly how to use these applications; simple videos for this are available online, on the websites themselves, and/or on sites like YouTube.

- Quizlet and Kahoot. These are websites/apps that allow you to set quizzes for your students; these quizzes can be completed either individually or in teams (Sari et al., 2020). They can be done before classes to review prior content or to see what your students already know; during classes in competitions to boost engagement and/or to see how much of the content your students are retaining; and after classes to see what they have retained from the lesson or as homework.

Platforms you can use

- Plickers. This is a website/application that allows students to answer questions by holding up printed copies of QR codes. You input questions and potential answers onto the site; they hold up their QR codes and, depending what angle they hold the QR code, a different answer is provided. You scan the QR codes and it records all of their answers under their individual names (names can be linked to QR code) (Krause et al., 2017).
- Thinglink. This is a website/app that allows you to upload images with links to information embedded in them. This can be used to expose students to content before a lesson, during a lesson, or as a part of some inquiry-based learning and to support students with research projects (Appasamy, 2018).
- Nearpod. This is a platform that allows students to have access to a lesson (sort of like an interactive PPT), which you can lead them through or they can lead themselves through (Fimala et al., 2022).
- Zoom and Tencent. These are interactive platforms that allow you to host lessons and live video/written chat. They also have storage functions through which you can share resources. These platforms have many functions, such as mute, screen share, video share, chat box, raise hand, and many more (Zhang & Lu, 2021).

Table 2.1 Matching teacher needs with platform functions

What you want the platform to do	What kind of function will do this	Examples of some platforms or apps which do this
Helps teachers create resources easily (Huang et al., 2020).	A function that allows teachers to create lessons, quizzes, questions, task sheets, and other materials within it.	Quizlet, Kahoot, Thinglink, Nearpod, Plickers, and many more.
Helps teachers manage resources easily (Huang et al., 2020).	A function that allows teachers to create shared storage areas, which students can also access.	Quizlet, Kahoot, Thinglink, Zoom, Tencent, and many more.
Publishes notifications to students (Huang et al., 2020).	A function that links to emails and/or sends updates to students.	Quizlet, Kahoot, Thinglink, Zoom, Tencent, and many more.
Manages and organises students (Huang et al., 2020).	A function that automatically grades assessments/quizzes.	Quizlet, Kahoot, Plickers, and many more.

(*Continued*)

Platforms you can use

Table 2.1 (Continued)

What you want the platform to do	What kind of function will do this	Examples of some platforms or apps which do this
	A function that allows teachers to create share files, which students can access.	Zoom, Tencent, and many more.
Allows students to obtain resources (Huang et al., 2020).	A function that allows students to access materials, quizzes, and lessons either independently or during classes.	Quizlet, Kahoot, Thinglink, Nearpod, Tencent, Zoom, and many more.
Has functions whereby students can participate in learning activities simply and easily (Huang et al., 2020).	Functions such as "enter a code to see resources" and pre-loaded quizzes that the students can attempt.	Quizlet, Kahoot, Nearpod, and many more.
	Live interactive platforms that allow students to be moved from a whole class group into break out rooms to collaborate.	Zoom, Tencent, and many more.
Provides quick and easy methods of communication (Huang et al., 2020).	Live interaction platforms allow this, especially ones with a chat box function.	Zoom, Tencent, and many more.
Gives feedback to parents (Huang et al., 2020).	If parents' email address is linked to the login, then they can get updates for classes and lessons from the apps used. Overall, I would recommend doing this yourself; it allows you to tailor the feedback more specifically.	Quizlet, Kahoot Nearpod, Zoom, Tencent, and many more.
Offers interactive elements for students to participate in (Hrastinski, 2009).	Platforms and apps that give students free rein or at least some freedom over lesson progression and the ability to complete quizzes or compete in groups to answer questions.	Quizlet, Kahoot, Nearpod, and many more.
Allows visual elements to be embedded within the lesson (David & Glore, 2010).	Live interaction platforms that allow you to screen share allow this.	Zoom, Tencent, Thinglink, Nearpod, and many more.
24/7 support available to help solve problems that arrive (Roca et al., 2006).	Bigger companies with a larger market share of the users will have these in place.	Quizlet, Kahoot Nearpod, Zoom, Thinglink, Tencent, and many more.

What I use

So, just to be clear, what I use does not mean that these are what you should use. When I currently teach online, I work with a class that has 24 students in it; you need to consider what will support your students to best meet their learning goals and your teaching style. If I were teaching 30 students, or 1-to-1 classes, I may use a different combination of platforms and applications.

Here we go. I use a combination of Quizlet, Zoom, and Nearpod. I use Quizlet mostly to assess key facts and see where students have not understood something/I have explained it poorly. I also use it for seeing student progression data. I use Nearpod to guide students through lessons; I occasionally allow them to guide themselves and act as a support for them where necessary. I use Zoom to give lesson input, communicate, discuss ideas, create break out groups, and share files. I also use the screen share function on Zoom to demonstrate how to use any applications before we use them and to model or demonstrate activities where necessary. I have and do use Plickers from time to time, but only usually with smaller classes, as I have found scanning the QR codes online can be challenging.

Conclusion

Online platforms, applications, and websites are the technological tools that you can use to deliver your lessons and content and to support your students. When used carefully and properly, they can lead to an engaging and fruitful learning environment. When poorly selected and not taken advantage of, the online classroom suffers.

There are a range of key functions that a platform can have that you should look out for. These include functions that help you manage resources, notify students, organise students, share resources with students, enable student participation, provide quick and easy communication, give feedback to parents, and track student performance (Huang et al., 2020).

To enhance online learning, we need to enhance student participation (Hrastinski, 2009). One way of doing this is to use platforms that allow the implementation of visual elements (David & Glore, 2010). Another way is to look out for functions that support student interaction, such as break out rooms or chat boxes.

Platforms you can use

There are many things to avoid when selecting an online platform. Asarbakhsh and Sandars (2013) believed that technological issues negatively impacted user satisfaction. Another study found that "network congestion" negatively impacted student satisfaction the most (Chen et al., 2020). As such, avoid platforms that have little or no support and/or a reputation for going down regularly. It is also important to avoid overly complicated platform designs that are difficult to use, and platforms that are inaccessible to many devices.

Online learning satisfaction is impacted mostly by the perceived usefulness and quality of the course; the degree of expected achievement; the quality of the platform; and the website service availability. As such, online teachers should select platforms that do not go down regularly and allow them to demonstrate course quality in simple ways (Roca et al., 2006).

Some platforms that can be used are Quizlet, Kahoot, Thinglink, Nearpod, Zoom, and Tencent. There are many others. As an online teacher, it is your responsibility to research ones that best suit your students and your teaching context. Use the research findings presented here to select the ones that will do this for you.

Key takeaways

- *Online platforms are websites, programs, or applications you can use to teach your online class.*
- *Great platforms help you create and manage resources; manage and share resources with students; notify students; allows students to participate easily; have simple communication methods; and track student performance (Huang et al., 2020).*
- *Enhancing student learning requires the enhancement of student participation (Hrastinski, 2009). Find a platform that allows you to increase participation through functions such as break out rooms/ interactive elements and imagery.*
- *Avoid platforms that are well known for being "down" or having broken/problematic features; this has the highest degree of impact on user satisfaction (Asarbakhsh & Sandars, 2013; Chen et al., 2020).*

- *Avoid platforms that have complicated designs and no customer support (Chen et al., 2020).*
- *There are many platforms that you can use, including Quizlet, Kahoot, Nearpod, Thinglink, Zoom, and Tencent.*
- *As a teacher, you should search the internet to find platforms that meet your own and your students' needs.*
- *Online learning user satisfaction is said to be most impacted by four determinants (Roca et al., 2006):*
  - *Perceived usefulness and quality of the course.*
  - *The degree of expected achievement.*
  - *The quality of the platform.*
  - *The website service.*
- *When searching for appropriate platforms, be mindful of the research and find what works the best for you.*
- *It is okay and sometimes even a great idea to combine platforms.*

Bibliography

Appasamy, P. (2018). Fostering student engagement with digital microscopic images using ThingLink, an image annotation program. *Journal of College Science Teaching*, 16–21.

Asarbakhsh, M., & Sandars, J. (2013). E-learning: The essential usability perspective. *The Clinical Teacher*, 47–50.

Chen, T., Peng, L., Yin, X., Rong, J., Yang, J., & Cong, G. (2020). Analysis of user satisfaction with online education platforms in China during the COVID-19 pandemic. *Healthcare, 8*(3), 200.

David, A., & Glore, P. (2010). The impact of design and aesthetics on usability, credibility, and learning in an online environment. *Online Journal of Distance Learning Administration, 13*(4).

Fimala, Y., Alwi, N. A., Miaz, Y., & Darmansyah, D. (2022). Blended learning LKPD development based on learning using Nearpod applications for integrated learning in elementary school. *Journal of Innovation in Educational and Cultural Research*, 97–105.

Hrastinski, S. (2009). A theory of online learning as online participation. *Computers & Education*, 78–82.

Huang, R., Zhang, M., Shen, Y., Tian, Y., & Zeng, H. (2020). Research on the core elements of an ultra-large-scale internet education organization: Case analysis of online education effectively supporting "School is Out, but Class is On." *Requests for Audio-Visual Equipment*, 10–19.

Krause, J. M., O'Neil, K., & Dauenhauer, B. (2017). Plickers: A formative assessment tool for K – 12 and PETE professionals. *Strategies*, 30–36.

Roca, J. C., Chiu, C. M., & Martínez, F. J. (2006). Understanding e-learning continuance intention: An extension of the Technology Acceptance Model. *International Journal of Human-computer Studies*, 683–696.

Sari, D. E., Ftriani, S. A., & Saputra, R. C. (2020). Active and interactive learning through Quizlet and Kahoot. *Active and Interactive Learning Through Quizlet and Kahoot*, 118–120.

Zhang, Z., & Lu, Y. (2021). Online education improvement using environment-based design approach. *International Journal of Systematic Innovation*, 5–12.

Classroom management online

An old co-worker of mine was struggling with classroom management and attended a training session where he was given some classroom management tools to try out. After putting them into practice, his exact words to me were: "I did exactly what they said would work, and it worked, I can't believe how easy it is." I never forgot what he said to me and know it to be true myself. I hope the tools you find here are as useful for you as I have seen them be for other teachers and myself.

This chapter goes over the common problems that teachers face in an online classroom, including how to set rules appropriately, motivate students, and use positive reinforcement properly in this context. This also includes the different types of reward systems that may be appropriate. The conclusion is that classroom management is in place for the teacher to set up an optimal learning environment for the students, and that a positive approach typically works best.

Aims of the chapter

By the end of this chapter, you will know:

- What is online classroom management?
- What are the benefits of classroom management?
- Why do students misbehave and how can we address these reasons in an online classroom?

- *How to create rules for the online classroom.*
- *How positive reinforcement can help you manage your class.*

Done right vs. done wrong

The following are two scenarios of online classrooms. Scenario A is an example in which the teacher has not developed any classroom management strategies or routines. Scenario B is an example where the teacher has developed these. The results are wildly different; think about how the teachers, students, and parents feel before, during, and after these lessons. For this example, it is written as though you, the reader, are the teacher delivering the class.

Scenario A

Picture this – a teacher is sitting behind their computer screen; all is peaceful and tranquil. However, that is all about to change. With a quick double click on the live video chat platform, a class is about to begin. As soon as it loads, mayhem, chaos, and disorder of the least productive or constructive kind are revealed. The students are all speaking and shouting at the same time, making it impossible to discern anything anyone is saying. Moreover, it makes the platform a little slower, which causes the already struggling laptop to freeze for a few seconds (secretly, the teacher does not mind the freeze; it offers a moment of silence).

After shouting down the microphone and messaging 15 sets of parents, the students are listening and ready to receive some lesson input. As the teacher starts to speak, a student unmutes their microphone and starts making silly noises. The teacher mutes the student's microphone and continues (the rest of the class is laughing; they all begin to imitate this). It takes 15 gruelling minutes to get the students to stop this. Exhausted and demoralised, the teacher realises there are only 10 minutes of the class left (relief and disappointment wash over them with the realisation that soon, freedom will come, even though the students have been failed and have learnt nothing other than to treat teachers and their peers with a little bit less respect).

The teacher finally gets the students to understand what they are meant to be learning, but it is too late. The lesson needs to end, and the teacher assigns

Classroom management online

some homework that the students will not be able to do – but don't worry, their parents will do it for them (which gives false information about the students' levels, annoys the parents who may/may not be paying the teacher's salary, and teaches the children nothing other than how to shirk their responsibility). The teacher turns off their computer, defeated and in doubt of their career, thinking: "What could I have done to make that lesson go well?"

Scenario B

A smile appears on the teacher's face; it is that time again. The laptop is opened gleefully, knowing that some real growth and development in the students is about to start (and some fun had at the same time!). The teacher double clicks the live video chat and the students are all talking. The teacher puts their hands on their head and the students all follow suit (the faster students get rewarded). All of them are listening now; they are told that they have 5 minutes before class starts and they should get their materials ready to show upon the lesson beginning.

The lesson timer goes off, microphones are muted, and hands go on heads. The teacher says "1, 2, 3, show me" and unmutes all microphones. They hold up their materials and say "1, 2, show you." Perfect – they are ready to start. Microphones go back on mute for now and materials are put behind the students, out of their reach.

As the context is set, questions are asked to elicit ideas and information and students raise their hands to answer and share their thoughts. One student gets out of their chair and the teacher says, "Sitting nicely please," and points to an image of a student sitting nicely behind them on the wall. The student sits back down and is praised for listening. The teacher runs through the input stage of the lesson; there are plenty of opportunities for students to participate both individually and through plenary. By this point, there are few to no disruptions: peaceful.

Next, students are instructed to do their gap-fill activity and to attempt the extension if they have time. They work quietly and only raise their hand to ask for help. After this, they know the "mark your own" routine that is in place; the teacher runs through the worksheet with them and makes corrections where necessary. Teams are rewarded for good effort and behaviour on the reward system on the wall behind the teacher.

Finally, the class is wrapped up with a quick plenary; the students have got it! The teacher assigns the homework that they can and will complete themselves (this shows if they have met the learning goals, reassures parents, and teaches the students that they can take responsibility for their own tasks and complete them properly.) Time to breathe easy, confident in the decision to have your online classroom well supported by student-led rules, routines, visual aids, reward systems, and positive reinforcement.

> One of these two options is preferable to the other. Teachers have a tremendous amount of control over classroom management and the setting up of a productive learning environment. This is incredibly important to remember. To get us started, let's look at what classroom management is and what it means.

Introduction

Classroom management is an extremely important part of a teacher's job. It can be the aspect of class that boosts morale and creates interconnectedness, or it can be the thing that causes absolute chaos, negativity, and constant disruption.

First of all, what even is it?

Classroom management is an ever-evolving and developing concept. Emmer and Sabornie (2015, pp. 7, 8) state "it is apparent that it would be difficult to encapsulate the diversity of classroom management components within a single succinct definition." This does not mean it is totally without definition, though. Henley (2010) defines classroom management as the process by which teachers reduce the frequency and degree of disruptions, as well as their ability to set up learning environments where knowledge can be attained and deepened optimally. Cangelosi (2013) talks about classroom management in the context of keeping students on task while having them learning and cooperating with each other and the teacher. Di Giulio (2007) puts forward the importance of positivity and its benefits in the context of classroom management.

Based on these, we will loosely define classroom management as the process by which the teacher ensures the classroom stays on task, positive, and productive, while working to reduce distractions/disruptions and maximise student self-behaviour management, leading to the establishment of an optimal learning environment.

There is a wide range of ways that you can manage your online classroom. Some great news for teachers with experience in a physical/traditional classroom is that many of the tools you used in the physical setting can be slightly altered to be suitable and fitting for the online classroom.

An additional study from 2020 that took place in Indonesia is worth mentioning. It indicated that rules, routines, proper relationships, and motivating and engaging students were effective tools for online classroom management (Lathifah et al., 2020).

Throughout this chapter, as you are exposed to research and practical strategies, think about how you can apply them to your online practice and how your students could take value from what you read.

What are the benefits of classroom management?

While there are many benefits that stem from a well-managed classroom, we are going to focus of three key areas: teacher burnout, student progress, and classroom environment impacts.

Teacher burnout

A meta-analysis of 16 studies showed that teachers' classroom management self-efficacy (CMSE) significantly correlated with three indicators of teacher burnout: emotional exhaustion, depersonalisation, and (lowered) personal accomplishment. Teachers with high levels of CMSE are less likely to experience burnout on these three dimensions; equally, teachers with low levels of CMSE are more likely to experience them. Basically, if teachers believe that they are competent with regard to classroom management, which is based on experience, perception of self and perception from others, then they experience greater wellbeing, enjoy their job more, and last longer in their profession (Aloe et al., 2013).

As a teacher, you need to consider your own wellbeing; it is a profession well known for its challenging nature. This being the case, you need to build your own confidence and belief in your classroom management practice. Like the research suggests, you can do this by improving your competency with regard to your classroom management skills. Before we address this in more detail, let's look at some more benefits.

Students and the classroom environment

While it is important to consider the benefits with regard to teacher well-being and burnout, it is also deeply important to consider the students and the classroom environment. As such, here are some drawn from Manning's book *Classroom Management: Models, Applications, and Cases* (2014).

- The creation of a controlled learning environment, ensuring objectives are achieved.
- The creation of a safe learning environment where students are not at risk of harming themselves (e.g. playing around on computer chairs, or leaning back is not safe).
- Prevention of undesirable behaviour that can lead to missed learning goals, dangerous circumstances, and frustration for all.
- The overcoming of undesirable behaviour, leading to more engaged and focused learners (not to mention teacher wellbeing!).
- Promotion of positivity and a positive learning environment within which students thrive.

(Manning, 2014)

These sound great, and they are. So, clearly, these are solid reasons to be concerned with classroom management. One of the most important things to remember is, you are there for the students; they are not there for you. Often, it is important not so much why you want "good behaviour," but rather why the students are not exhibiting it. This means that rather than simply extinguishing the same problem every day, go to the source. Perhaps a student is misbehaving because they do not understand the tasks and need scaffolds; discovering this is often more important than simply stopping the student from shouting out or playing with something on their desk.

Why do students misbehave?

The list of reasons why students might misbehave is long, and much of it is somewhat beyond a teacher's ability to find out (without the dedication of a great deal of time, resources, and effort). That being said, think about the reasons you do not pay attention or why you might be bored during an online training session. The reasons you might be off task or doing something you shouldn't be are likely to be similar to the reasons your students manifest these actions. Reed and Kirkpatrick figured these out a long time ago:

1   Boredom (too easy/not interesting/irrelevant curriculum).
2   Lack of understanding (poor support structures).
3   Lack of energy or effort needed (no freedom to move around at all).
4   Lack of reward system or praise (no immediate payoff).
5   Lack of confidence (this could be considered self-efficacy).
6   Poor rapport with the teacher.
7   Lack of classroom rules (or no consequences).
8   Distractions.

(Reed & Kirkpatrick, 1998)

After discussing the causes of misbehaviour with hundreds of teachers, I have found that almost all of the problems they face fall under one of or a combination of the above reasons students misbehave. Next, let's look at some of the ways to address these causes of misbehaviour.

How can we address these reasons in an online classroom?

Addressing causes can be complicated, and you will need to somewhat approach this on a case-by-case basis. This does not mean there are standard tools and approaches that are "generally" good practice. The whole purpose of identifying the causes is to figure out the potential interventions or procedures you can follow to resolve the issues, so let's look at some.

Table 3.1 Causes of misbehaviour, solutions to this, and how this may look in a real online classroom

Cause of misbehaviour	Potential solution	How it might look in your online classroom
Boredom	Tailor lessons to students' ability and use relatable materials. The lesson and curriculum need to be relevant and interesting (Macklem, 2015).	You would have differentiated tasks (see the differentiation section in Chapter 11) for students to complete, and the lesson would have a relatable theme (perhaps a cartoon character they know would be embedded).

(Continued)

Table 3.1 (Continued)

Cause of misbehaviour	Potential solution	How it might look in your online classroom
Lack of understanding	Scaffold lessons properly (Keast, 2020) and give clear instructions and demonstrations. Poorly delivered instructions result in lower achievement for students (El Kemma, 2019).	Your online lesson will begin the concept at its most basic form and build from there. Avoid assuming students already know the information. Provide a range of materials to learn from (imagery, video resources, demonstrations).
Lack of energy or effort needed/ no freedom to move around	Introduce more kinaesthetic activities. Students who learn better through a kinaesthetic approach are more likely to misbehave when required to sit still for extended periods of time (Ginnis, 2002).	Your lesson will have multiple moments where you have the students stand up from their computer chairs. You will have action-based response games throughout the lesson.
Lack of reward system or praise	Offer praise and rewards for good behaviours (Di Giulio, 2007).	You will regularly praise students when they manifest desirable behaviours and have a reward system on the wall behind you, visible within your camera frame.
Lack of confidence	Boost students up through positive praise (Di Giulio, 2007).	Showing the class a good piece of work on screen share, which a student has completed, is a good way to do this.
Poor rapport with the teacher	Have "get to know each other" segments to your lessons – show interest in your students (Rogers & Smith, 2011). Use of humour can impact this, too (Lathifah et al., 2020).	Start your lessons with a relatable joke or imitation of a character the students know. Regularly ask the students appropriate questions about their lives and share appropriate information about your own.
Lack of classroom rules	Establish rules and stick to them (Dabell, 2017).	You will have a visible set of rules on the wall behind you, which you can point to when necessary.
Distractions	Use interesting materials that students can relate to and see a use for knowing (Mayer, 2002). Also, avoid toys and things laying around on the students' desks.	You will instruct parents and students to ensure there are no toys or objects on the computer desk that can distract their children.

Considering your own classroom, your own personality, and the nature of the problems that are manifesting in your online classroom, you can begin to build your own solutions. It is important to remember these fundamental causes of misbehaviour and that the student is rarely attempting to sabotage a lesson; more often than not, they are calling out for you to solve one of the issues discussed earlier.

One of the best ways to establish a necessary level of order in the classroom is to have rules that are well known and understood by your students and yourself. The next section will fully equip you to develop rules like these in your online classroom.

Rules in the online classroom

Setting rules at the start of a lesson is fundamental to proper classroom management (Lathifah et al., 2020). Doing this sets your expectations, allows the students to set their expectations, and gives them and you a framework within which to monitor behaviour.

Rules are one of the most important and integral aspects of the online classroom. It is argued that they are the backbone of the classroom and the most important aspect of governing behaviour. They can be linked to a varjety of important areas, including reward systems, the formal curriculum, the hidden curriculum, and promoting a positive environment. A recent review of the literature indicated that the two most important characteristics of effective rule creation and use are to teach the rules to the students and to tie rules to positive and negative consequences (Alter & Haydon, 2017).

Positive and negative rules

Positive rules are connected to promoting a positive online classroom environment; these would include rules that focus heavily on positive behaviour and encouraging it. Examples of these are "listen to others, always try, and be helpful." These kinds of rules move students' minds towards positivity and as such influence the classroom environment in the same way (Scott et al., 2007).

Negative rules are connected to hindering the creation of a positive classroom environment; these include a heavy focus on rules that promote too much "no" and not enough "do." For example, a rules list that states "do not speak, do not shout, and do not be late" promotes negativity and can cause students to feel demoralised.

Table 3.2 Examples of positive and negative rules

Positive rules examples	Negative rules examples
◆ Be safe and tidy. ◆ Be clean. ◆ Always listen to others. ◆ Always try. ◆ Sit nicely. ◆ Be respectful. ◆ Speak clearly and nicely.	◆ Do not be mean. ◆ Do not shout out. ◆ Do not sit stupidly. ◆ No talking. ◆ Do not daydream. ◆ Never be lazy. ◆ Do not play. ◆ Do not fight. ◆ Do not argue.

These are not necessarily the rules you should use; they are simply some rule examples. As stated previously, you can work with your students to figure out what rules are best for your learning space.

Student-centred rules

Student-centred rules are when you allow the students to create and develop their own rules. A study of a Grade 2 class showed that this method decreased the frequency of off-task behaviour (Rosebrock, 2007). When having students work with you to navigate the rules they want, they will develop a keener understanding of the importance and purpose of the rules.

This process can be time-consuming; however, it should still be encouraged as it tends to reap these benefits. Students who are allowed to create rules with their teacher feel as though their opinions are valued; students' awareness of the importance of collaboration is raised; students feel more responsible for maintaining the rules and abiding by them; and, in some cases, students will self- and peer-manage misbehaviour (Brady et al., 2011).

If you are limited on time and have some key rules that you really want to be in the lesson, you can pre-decide some rules and have the students brainstorm to add on some rules. This combats the problem of time management and still takes some of positive results of student-created rules.

Last bits on rules

- KISS rules.
  Keep It Simple for Students rules are rules that are made as simple as possible. These are easy to remember, easy to utilise, and deeply clear. An example of one is "be kind" instead of "make sure you do kind things to the students around you in the class." Long, complicated rules can lead to confused students (especially with younger ages) (Whitaker et al., 2019)
- Visual aids.
  Visual aids can and should be used to support rules (Alter & Haydon, 2017). You can and should use flashcards for your online classroom. You can stick them to the wall behind your camera; this makes them clear for students to see. On some platforms you can upload images of rules to the platform, which is also effective. Another good option, if possible, is to create a rules reminder sheet that students and parents can print out and stick on their walls at home, by the computer.
- Using teams.
  Using teams and team point systems can be an effective way to get the students to self-impose and regulate the rules (Dutton Tillery et al., 2010). Just be careful that the students don't start bullying each other or making each other feel marginalised because of behavioural problems that some students may face.

The best online teachers I ever observed were persistent, consistent, and insistent about the rules. They did not tyrannise their classroom; they were just fair. While enforcing rules, remain calm and act rationally without showing any upset. Questioning students to lead them to the conclusion that they have misbehaved is a good way of doing this: "Is shouting at the microphone good?" "Why do we speak nicely in class?" Questions that lead the student to reflect on their behaviour convey meaning far better than "Greg! STOP SHOUTING!" Remember – you are the students' role model here; how you respond gives them a template of how people should act.

Remember, these are your students and you know them far better than I do or any other teacher could. Take value from the ideas here but build them into your own. See what works well and what doesn't.

Positive classroom management

Positive reinforcement is a great tool for online classroom management. You can offer praise and rewards to students who follow the rules and try hard at their work. Using a reward system you have developed with your students is often effective (see Chapter 4, on student engagement, for more on reward systems).

Positive classroom management is all about the establishment of a positive learning space and the avoidance of overemphasis on negative consequences. A positive learning space is one in which students feel safe and confident to take risks and make mistakes. They need to feel respected and equal. The needs of all students, both high and low attainers, need to be met (typically through differentiation; see "Differentiation" in Chapter 11 to learn more), and feedback should be given in a positive and productive manner (Ollerton, 2004).

Operant conditioning

Operant conditioning is B. F. Skinner's idea that behaviour is crafted by consequences. Behaviours that are rewarded and treated positively will emerge more often, while behaviours that are punished and treated negatively emerge less (Staddon & Cerutti, 2003). While this is an incomplete idea and does not take into account the individual within, there is some practicality in knowing how this may be used in your online practice.

How you can use this

This can be applied to a classroom easily. When students behave in a desirable way, reward them according to your reward system, e.g. give them a star. When students behave in an undesirable way, you can remove a star. A word of caution – online classrooms that do not focus heavily enough on positive reinforcement and too much on negative reinforcement tend to have demoralised students. We advise avoiding negativity as much as possible; rather than removing stars, give students reflection time.

One good way to reprimand students without it feeling negative is to have a teacher vs. students reward system. If they are bad – you receive the point; if they are good, they receive the point. This removes the feeling of having their hard-earned points taken away. Alternatively, you could have a reward system where the students are climbing a mountain, running away from a bear. If they behave poorly, the bear gets closer. When the bear catches them, they start again.

Proximity praise

Proximity praise is when you praise a student who is expressing desirable behaviours to demonstrate to students within their proximity a good behaviour. Proximity praise often impacts whole class behaviour (Gable et al., 2009), especially online because all of the students can see each other easily.

How you can use this

If a student is misbehaving, pick a student who is not and reward them for doing the thing you want the misbehaving student to do. This demonstrates to the student who is misbehaving that the correct behaviours will receive praise and potentially even rewards. For example, if X is playing with a pencil, you could give Y a point on the reward system and say, "Y, that is wonderful, you are sitting so nicely and you are not playing with your pencil." This way the whole class (including X) knows that right now, it is not time to play with a pencil, and if they do not play with one, they may get rewarded.

Relationships

A positive online learning environment needs good relationships. If there is animosity in the air, focus is divided and students often become too shy to make mistakes. Students must also feel as though they have a good relationship with their teacher and their peers. One great way to build healthy relationships with students is using humour and jokes in the classroom (Lathifah et al., 2020). Let's look at another great way to do this.

A 2018 study showed that greeting students positively at the classroom door reduced behavioural issues and increased academic engagement time (Cook et al., 2018). I recently wrote an article for TES about this titled "5 Positive Greeting Ideas for Online Lessons." It became their most read online article that week and has repeatedly reached this status since. In my article, I suggest five ways you can do this in your online classroom:

Classroom management online

- Positively welcome the students.
  - Simply greeting them politely and showing interest in them is fine.
- Use filters and add-ons.
  - Like apps that give turn you into a dragon or give you funny ears.
- Setting up your own weekly welcome video.
  - Having this play on screen share gives the students something to do; you could have a video simply showing some things you did that week, shopping, etc. This lets them feel like they know you more.
- Using lesson starter games.
  - Especially ones that let the whole class win something (like slightly less homework!).
- Lesson starter songs.
  - Perfect with the younger students and something the early years teachers out there will be very used to.

(Macur, 2021)

The next section reviews a few key additional points on classroom management that will be covered in more details in Chapter 4.

Last bits classroom management

There are three other points that are worth adding in here, however; we will go into more detail about these points in Chapter 4. Having said that, the three additional great methods of managing a class are:

- Grouping the students into teams.
  Having students work together is a great way to keep them on task and supported. Two great ways to drop this into your online teaching practice are to use break out rooms or set group projects. A word of warning – if you set group projects, make sure you have clear roles for the students to adopt; otherwise, one student tends to end up doing all of the work (Burke, 2011).
- Keeping students engaged.
  An engaged class are far more likely to be on task and cooperative. They may still misbehave, but if they are engaged, they are much easier to bring back on track (Wentzel, 2021). Simply stopping the lesson and explaining that we cannot continue unless they are following the rules that were agreed upon works well with an engaged class.

- Motivating students.
  Typically, reward systems land nicely in here, as well as goal setting (Wentzel, 2021). There are many different types ways of approaching these areas. I suggest moving to Chapter 4, on engaging students, to find out more.

Next, we have a short conclusion to wrap up the ideas covered in this chapter.

Conclusion

Classroom management is the method by which teachers create a learning environment that has optimal levels of order and freedom for students to learn in the most effective ways. There are many benefits that come from proper classroom management, such as reduced levels of teacher burnout (Aloe et al., 2013), better meeting of learning goals, reduction of distraction and misbehaviour, increased student engagement, and a safer learning environment (Manning, 2014). The reasons students misbehave revolve largely around boredom, poor relationships, and a lack of understanding (Reed & Kirkpatrick, 1998). Ways of addressing this include tailoring, scaffolding, and gearing lessons towards interests for students; break out rooms can be utilised and props on the wall are essential.

Rules are one of the cornerstones of a classroom (Lathifah et al., 2020). As teachers, we should focus on positive rules and have the students develop them as a class; this encourages ownership of them and can improve their effectiveness (Rosebrock, 2007).

Finally, using positivity in the classroom is beneficial as it helps to build a thriving and positive classroom environment. Approaches like proximity praise tend to work well and can even impact the whole class (Gable et al., 2009).

Key takeaways

- *A properly managed classroom will reduce the chances of teacher burnout, emotional exhaustion, depersonalisation, and (lowered) personal accomplishment (Aloe et al., 2013).*
- *A properly managed classroom will benefit students through the creation of a controlled learning environment; the creation of a*

safe learning environment; preventing undesirable behaviours; and creating a more engaging and positive learning environment (Manning, 2014).
- *Students usually misbehave for the following reasons: boredom, a lack of understanding, a lack of energy or effort needed, a lack of reward system or praise, a lack of confidence, poor rapport with the teacher, a lack of classroom rules, and distractions (Reed & Kirkpatrick, 1998).*
- *These problems can be solved by using relatable contexts, differentiating materials, having students move around and stand up, sharing examples of student work that is good, establishing rules and having them visible on the wall behind you, and praising good behaviour.*
  - *These solutions can be supported through the use of key platform functions like screen share, break out rooms, and chat box functions.*
- *Rules should be established at the start of lessons (Lathifah et al., 2020). They should be student-created and focused on positive language (Rosebrock, 2007).*
- *Having students central to the rule creation process leads to a range of benefits (Cangelosi, 2013).*
- *Positive reinforcement should be used where possible (Ollerton, 2004); tools like proximity praise and calling on students who are behaving well are great ways to do this (Gable et al., 2009).*
- *Building relationships through humour (Lathifah et al., 2020), showing interest, and positive greetings when students arrive are effective. Teachers can also use filters and games to start lessons to set a positive tone (Macur, 2021).*
- *Grouping, reward systems, and engaging students are also essential tools for classroom management (see Chapter 4).*

Bibliography

Aloe, A. M., Amo, L. C., & Shanahan, M. E. (2013). Classroom management self-efficacy and burnout: A multivariate meta-analysis. *Educational Psychology Review*, 101–126.

Alter, P., & Haydon, T. (2017). Characteristics of effective classroom rules: A review of the literature. *The Journal of the Teacher Education Division of the Council for Exceptional Children*, 114–127.

Brady, K., Forton, M. B., & Porter, D. (2011). *Rules in school: Teaching discipline in the responsive classroom*. Center for Responsive Schools.

Burke, A. (2011). Group work: How to use groups effectively. *Journal of Effective Teaching*, 87–95.

Cangelosi, J. S. (2013). *Classroom management strategies: Gaining and maintaining students' cooperation*. John Wiley & Sons.

Cook, C. R., Fiat, A., Larson, M., Daikos, C., Slemrod, T., Holland, E. A., et al. (2018). Positive greetings at the door: Evaluation of a low-cost, high-yield proactive classroom management strategy. *Journal of Positive Behavior Interventions*, 149–159.

Dabell, J. (2017). Creating rules in your classroom. *SecEd*, *30*, 10.

Di Giulio, R. C. (2007). *Positive classroom management: A step-by-step guide to helping students succeed*. Corwin Press.

Dutton Tillery, A., Varjas, K., Meyers, J., & Collins, A. S. (2010). General education teachers' perceptions of behavior management and intervention strategies. *Journal of Positive Behavior Interventions*, 86–102.

El Kemma, A. (2019). Giving effective instructions in EFL classrooms. *International Journal for Innovation Education and Research*, 74–92.

Emmer, E., & Sabornie, E. J. (2015). *Handbook of classroom management*. Routledge.

Gable, R. A., Hester, P. H., Rock, M. L., & Hughes, K. G. (2009). Back to basics: Rules, praise, ignoring, and reprimands revisited. *Intervention in School and Clinic*, 195–205.

Ginnis, P. (2002). *Raise classroom achievement with strategies for every learner*. Crown House Publishing Ltd.

Henley, M. (2010). *Classroom management: A proactive approach*. Prentice Hall.

Keast, D. (2020). The use of scaffolds to help improve students' success on persuasive term papers in an online music course. *International Journal on Innovations in Online Education*, *4*, 2.

Lathifah, Z. K., Helmanto, F., & Maryani, N. (2020). The practice of effective classroom management in COVID-19 time. *International Journal of Advanced Science and Technology*, 3263–3271.

Macklem, G. L. (2015). *Boredom in the classroom: Addressing student motivation, self-regulation, and engagement in learning*. Springer.

Macur, G. (2021, February 13). *5 positive greeting ideas for online lessons*. Retrieved August 10, 2021, from Times Educational Supplement: www.tes.com/news/5-positive-greeting-ideas-online-lessons

Manning, L. (2014). *Classroom management: Models, applications, and cases*. Pearson.

Mayer, R. E. (2002). Rote versus meaningful learning. *Theory into Practice*, 226–232.

Ollerton, M. (2004). *Creating positive classrooms*. Continuum.

Reed, D. F., & Kirkpatrick, C. (1998). Disruptive students in the classroom: A review of the literature. *Metropolitan Educational Research Consortium*, *1*, 1–90.

Rogers, J., & Smith, M. (2011). Demonstrating genuine interest in students' needs and progress. *Journal of Applied Research in Higher Education*, 6–14.

Rosebrock, S. E. (2007). *Implementation of student-created classroom rules that decreased off-task behavior in a second grade classroom*. Retrieved October 9, 2021, from Ohio Link ETD Center: https://etd.ohiolink.edu/apexprod/rws_olink/r/1501/10?clear=10&p10_accession_num=def1281637491

Scott, T. M., Park, K. L., Swain-Bradway, J., & Landers, E. (2007). Positive behavior support in the classroom: Facilitating behaviorally inclusive learning environments. *International Journal of Behavioral Consultation and Therapy*, 223–235.

Staddon, J. E., & Cerutti, D. T. (2003). Operant conditioning. *Annual Review of Psychology*, 115–144.

Wentzel, K. R. (2021). *Motivating students to learn* (5th ed.). Routledge.

Whitaker, T., Good, M. W., & Whitaker, K. (2019). *Classroom management from the ground up*. Routledge.

Online student engagement

Thinking about some of the online training I have been put through over the last few years, the worst part is when it is boring, unengaging, and your eyes get that heavy dry feeling that makes you feel as though sleep is looming. This is something worth considering as you develop your online teaching style. You do not want to be the teacher who puts their students through the mind-numbing experiences we have all had before.

This chapter looks at what student engagement is, why it is useful, and how you might achieve high levels of student engagement in your online classroom. It covers areas such as motivation, reward systems, and meaningful learning and touches on gamification. As always, research is integrated and made practical; also, tools that stood out to me from teaching online and observing teachers teaching online are included. The conclusion is that engaging students is essential to the proper functioning of an online classroom.

Aims of the chapter

By the end of this chapter, you will know:

- *What is student engagement?*
- *The benefits of student engagement.*
- *How to motivate students intrinsically vs. extrinsically.*
- *Different methods of applying reward systems.*
- *How interaction patterns can impact engagement.*
- *Context and meaningful learning and gamification.*

Online student engagement

Done right vs. done wrong

The following are two scenarios of online classrooms. Scenario A is an example where the teacher does not know how to engage their class, and what the consequences of this are. Scenario B is an example in which the teacher applies methods of engaging students, leading to a healthier, more productive, and enjoyable learning experience for all involved. While you read these two examples, think about how you would feel if you were the teacher of either of these two classes.

Scenario A

The lesson starts – no need to warm up. Why would teachers get the students moving before delving into the learning? No need to set the context; surely it doesn't matter if the information is embedded in relatable materials. Instead, the teacher just starts dictating the things the students are going to learn. As the teacher is talking, a wave of yawns falls from student to student.

No reward systems are introduced, and the teacher's monotone voice seems to go on forever; students have very little time for student-to-student interaction, and the chances of a group activity are practically nil.

Slowly but surely, the students' eyes get heavy; to entertain themselves, they begin to misbehave. The teacher stops the lesson to address the behaviour; the students slump more into boredom, and a sense of "how many minutes left?" falls over the class. Even the teacher can feel it.

The teacher screen shares some notes for the students to copy down; they do this like mindless drones, retaining next to none of the content they copy out (a photocopier does not remember the sheets that it scans).

The teacher decides to wrap the lesson up; they will use concept checking questions to see whether the students have retained and learnt the content that was delivered. One of two of them get a couple of the answers correct; the rest offer blank faces.

There is an end of class quiz the students need to complete before they can log out. The teacher knows all about self-grading quiz websites so uses one; the results fly in as the final student logs out. Almost none of the content has been learnt. The teacher lets out a groan of disappointment and thinks, "Why can't they just get it?"

Scenario B

The lesson starts; the teacher greets the students positively as they arrive and allocates them into teams. On the wall behind the teacher is an image of a mountain with four counters stuck to it (green, blue, brown, and purple), one colour for each team of students. To start class, there is a quick-fire recap of the previous lesson's content; the teacher asks a question, and if a student knows it, they need to stand up quickly. As they get answers correct, their team moves up.

The content for this class is introduced on screen share; there are images of relatable cartoon characters that the students know throughout the materials shared, to embed the content in a context the students find entertaining.

Students misbehave lightly from excitement, but the teacher stops this by holding one of the team magnets, indicating they have a chance to get points if they behave well.

The teacher sets team tasks and opens up break out rooms for students to collaborate in. As the teacher moves between the groups, the teacher turns their camera upside down so when they enter the class, the students get a good laugh. Positive reinforcement is applied thoroughly, and support is provided where necessary.

Students come back together from their break out groups to discuss what they did; all teams had slightly different tasks, so the discussion is rife. The teacher uses a range of vocal tones and models excited and engaged behaviour.

The lesson ends and the students complete the end of lesson quiz; content has been absorbed, and as students leave, they smile, wave, and say goodbye to their teacher.

The teacher smiles and thinks, "I can't wait for the next class!"

> *Granted, these two options demonstrate examples of classes that have gone awry or landed very nicely. The main point is, we are trying to move away from these negative examples that you are reading chapter after chapter and towards those that put a smile on your face and make you look forward to your next online class. Let's get started by looking at what we mean when we say "student engagement."*

Introduction

Throughout my career as a teacher and trainer, student engagement in the online learning environment has stood out to me as fundamentally important to the proper function of online learning. This has been confirmed by the hundreds of online lessons I have observed and repeatedly in discussions with other teachers and trainers. This is due to multiple reasons such as making lessons more enjoyable for all, and online education has higher rates of attention attrition than the traditional classroom (Angelino et al., 2007).

Student engagement has been a prominent area of attention in the literature since the 1990s. A literature review found that a robust collection of research indicated strong correlations between student involvement and positive outcomes across a range of desirable domains, such as student success and development, academic achievement, student satisfaction, persistence, and social engagement (Trowler, 2010). Trowler's literature review also touched upon a range of definitions for student engagement. Some of these are:

- How much students are engaging with activities that have been shown by higher education research to be related to high-quality learning objectives and outcomes (Krause & Coates, 2008).
- How much effort and what quality of effort students put into educational activities with desirable outcomes (Hu & Kuh, 2001).
- The efforts made by sector bodies and institutions to involve and empower students in the learning process (HEFCE, 2008).
- A combination of academic and non-academic aspects of student experience (Coates, 2007):
  - Active and collaborative learning;
  - Participation in challenging academic activities;
  - Formative communication with academic staff;
  - Involvement in enriching educational experiences;
  - Feeling legitimated and supported by university learning communities.

(Trowler, 2010, p. 7)

Considering these concepts, and in an attempt to wrap them up nicely together, we will define student engagement as the following: student engagement is the degree to which students are positively involved with the content, each other, the learning environment, and the instructor. Positive student engagement leads to the meeting of high-quality learning objectives. Negative student engagement leads to the hindering of these objectives, and no student engagement is where students are simply not clocked in.

What are the benefits of student engagement?

Backing up Trowler's literature review, Meyer (2014) argues that student engagement positively impacts satisfaction, performance, and academic achievement. What stands out quite clearly, from speaking to professionals and seeing it all in action, is that when students are engaged, a multiplicity of positive results are reaped:

- Students are more motivated so:
    - Time restrictions are more easily met.
    - They enjoy the lessons more.
    - You enjoy the lessons more (think back to teacher wellbeing and burnout rates in Chapter 3).
    - Parents see this and feel it is worth it.
    - Behavioural issues are reduced.

This list can go on for a long time. Seeing it clarifies the importance of student engagement in the online classroom. Moving on from these points, we will go on to look at what can be done.

What makes students disengage? There are many factors that cause student disengagement. These come from a range of stakeholders. Let's look at them in more detail.

Factors that cause engagement issues and how to potentially influence them

Disengaged students are often a result of a variety of factors. When speaking to teachers working online and industry professionals, the most commonly reported causes and whether they were easy to influence or difficult to influence were as follows.

Easy to influence

- Boring lessons – introduce more active activities (see Chapter 11).
- Content is not meaningful – use relatable cartoon characters when delivering content.
- They are demotivated – introduce reward systems.
- The content is too hard – use scaffolds and differentiate (see the differentiation section in Chapter 11).
- Your internet is not good enough – you need a strong connection to teach online.
- The lessons go too fast – slow things down and don't try to cram too much into a lesson; if you struggle to fit it all in, try flipped learning (see Chapter 11).
- The lessons go too slow – pick up the pace, introduce some group activities, increase the difficulty.

Hard to influence

- Parents in the background causing issues – a polite request can work.
- Noise outside their room – asking them to close windows or doors if possible can help (be aware of safeguarding policies; see Chapter 10).
- Things in their room – speaking to parents and requesting that distracting toys be removed can work.
- Weather – asking for windows to be closed can help.
- Internet issues – speaking to parents about this can sometimes get them to use a faster connection; alternatively, request that during lesson times, no downloading is going on.
- Lack of sleep – informing parents that the student is tired in lessons can help.
- Student is having a bad day/has got some bad news – other unpredictable factors like this can ruin a lesson; simply keeping the lesson entertaining can distract students from things that are bothering them outside of the context of the lesson.

As you can see, the easy-to-influence factors fall within the domain of the classroom, the lesson, the learning materials, and your teaching style. The factors that are hard to influence fall outside of our control areas as teachers. Having said that, it does not mean we cannot influence them at all.

Embedding motivational practice within your online lessons is a great way to keep students engaged. The next section will look at that in more detail.

How to motivate students intrinsically vs. extrinsically

Motivating students is a huge role played by online teachers. Through motivation, students are able to battle through difficult concepts, revise, and prepare for tests and exams properly, develop skills and knowledge at an incredibly fast rate, enjoy their time in a classroom, and achieve many of the desirable outcomes that teachers and students look for in a classroom (Wentzel & Miele, 2016).

Motivated learners are students who are happy to take part in the learning process; often, they are excited about and get a lot of fulfilment out of it. They usually exhibit the following characteristics:

- They are positive about tasks and take them on willingly.
- They are driven towards achievement and self-development.
- They have high aspirations.
- They are goal oriented and respond well to reward systems.
- They are tenacious and do not give up easily on difficult tasks.
- They do not become frustrated easily when learning difficult concepts.

(Wentzel, 2020)

It's the teacher's job! Motivating and driving students to work harder, achieve better grades, and believe in themselves is a key area that an online teacher needs to focus on. Students are often already shy about taking part in the online classroom as it is unfamiliar compared to a traditional classroom. It is a new environment, and it's the teacher's job to support them as they develop their drive. This is why all online teachers should study and understand the importance of motivation and positive reinforcement.

Taking a demotivated and demoralised student and turning them into a motivated positive student is not an easy task. It is possible, however. Online teachers must know why the student is unmotivated. Are they bored? Are they too challenged? Are they having problems at home? Teachers often need to identify what the cause of demotivation is before being able to tackle it.

So, how can a student be motivated? Let's look in more detail at the intrinsic and extrinsic motivating tools you have at your disposal.

Intrinsically motivating your students online

Intrinsic motivating factors are motivating forces that go on within a student; these are not a result of the outside world. Intrinsic motivation is extremely powerful but often quite difficult to influence. Developing students' intrinsic motivation will maximise the benefits reaped by students during lessons (Csikszentmihalyi, 2014).

Some reasons we develop intrinsic motivation are:

- A thirst for knowledge.
  - Students will, if interested in a topic, have a thirst to learn more about it.
- Self-affirmation.
  - Students will, if in the right environment, have an intrinsic drive for self-improvement.
- Self-improvement.
  - Students will also develop a desire to prove to themselves that they can do something.

(Csikszentmihalyi, 2014)

Attempting to develop a culture of intrinsic motivation development within your online practice is essential. Ways that have stood out to me over the years are:

- Encourage students to collaborate. Break out groups work well in the online classroom.
- Focus on positive motivation and positive reinforcement; this creates a feeling of excitement in the run up to the online lessons, making students look forward to and want to participate more.
- Set a future goal that is bigger than the small tasks that occur within a classroom, one that brings the group together and instils a group sense of belonging and teamwork. Perhaps the students can work towards completing a goal like the creation of a familiar cartoon character on the wall behind you; get creative with this one and see what works for your setting and students.

- Give your students the feeling of conscious choice. You should empower this feeling – let the online lesson be student led and student guided.
- Show interest in students' personal interests and encourage feedback. You could use warm-up activities where you each take a turn to share what you did that day/week.

Developing your own sense of classroom community, enabling students to create and nurture their own goals, and having a sense of love for learning can all also positively impact your students' intrinsic motivation. How else can students be motivated? Let's look at what extrinsic tools there are available for you to utilise.

Extrinsically motivating your students online

Extrinsic motivating factors are forces external to the student that motivate students to act. These are also extremely important and should be considered deeply when motivating students. Extrinsic motivation is much easier to utilise in your teaching practice than intrinsic motivation.

Online teachers have a lot of control over extrinsic motivation, and here are some examples of how you can use extrinsic motivation in your own online classes:

1. You are a source of extrinsic motivation. Students often seek recognition and praise for work produced. Give it to them.
2. Offer rewards such a stars and points; these can be incorporated into reward systems.
3. Have a student of the week award. This can also be of the lesson and/or month.
4. Let students know you will feed back their good work to their parents. This works on two fronts: they want their parents to hear they are great but also don't want their parents to potentially hear they were causing problems.
5. Show students that hard work will bring them good grades. This is connected to setting difficult but achievable tasks, and feeding back positively on work they put effort into.

(McLean, 2003)

There are many other ways you can use extrinsic motivation in an online classroom – be creative and think about the things that your students actually want. It can be an effective tool in keeping students on task/ achieving lesson objectives. A word of warning – over-focus on extrinsic motivation has been shown to diminish intrinsic motivation, so make sure you have a balance of the two within your practice (Fang et al., 2013). Having said that, this is something you have to decide once you know your students and how best to work with them (Benabou & Tirole, 2003).

The next section will look in detail at reward systems. These are one of the tools that can instantly enhance levels of engagement in a lesson; they also double up as a great classroom management tool!

What are different methods of applying reward systems?

This reward systems section is taken from interviewing and discussing best practice for reward system use with current teachers and teacher trainers working professionally.

Reward systems are simple: they are something that you set up in your online lessons and can be used to reward the students. The three kinds of reward system we will demonstrate to you are individual reward systems; team reward systems; and whole class reward systems. Use a combination of these and change them up from time to time; too often I have seen teachers using the same reward system for months, and it gets boring fast. On the flip side of that, completely changing it every lesson removes continuity. You need to watch your students and see how they engage with the reward system: whether it motivates them, if they respond when you offer points or some reward system-related incentive, and if they get excited and manage each other's behaviour/encourage each other to try hard so they can win. If they are responding as desired, continue using the reward system. If they are starting to lose interest, mix things up.

Some key things to remember are:

1. Be fair in your approach to using them.
2. Try to make them visual, e.g. having them on a board behind you or visible in your interactive platform/screen share.
3. Inform parents and even try to get them involved in motivating the students.

4 Let the students get involved with aspects of their creation – e.g. ask the class to design characters for themselves to have as their avatars.
5 Have prizes the students can win/rewards they want – you can even let them come up with their own rewards (within the confines of appropriateness).

Let's look at some examples of how this can be seen in your practice.

Individual reward systems

Individual reward systems are directed at students individually. They have full control of how well they proceed through them. These can include things like

1 Collecting stars on an interactive platform.
2 Climbing a mountain drawn on a board behind the teacher.
3 Win your way out of homework.

Individual reward systems are very good at supporting students individually. You can use them to motivate students through difficult tasks and in pairing with proximity praise (see Chapter 3).

Team reward systems

Team rewards systems are directed towards groups of students. Group and team performance and behaviour are great ways to ensure your online classroom runs smoothly and productively. The incentives can be similar to that of individual reward systems, but you can change the processes. Two examples are:

1 Split the class into four teams. Draw a mountain on the platform or on a board behind you, where good behaviour and taking part allow their team to climb the mountain. At a certain point, there is a reward.
2 Split the class into teams. Draw a table on the platform or on a board behind you and give stars to teams for good behaviour and participation. There can be prizes for the winners.

Team-based reward systems tend to get students more involved with behaviour management and motivation of each other. Be careful, though – you want to make this a positive process, so if possible avoid point removal, as this can cause rifts within the student teams.

Whole class reward systems

Whole class reward systems are directed at the entire class. The whole class must work together to achieve the reward.

A great example of this is a jigsaw reward system. You cut an image into pieces, and if the students are behaving and participating well, you stick one of the pieces up in view of the camera. Once the image is completed, the whole class gets a reward.

Whole class reward systems create a more connected feeling within your classroom as the students are all linked by a common goal.

Final note on reward systems

Reward systems are a great tool, but try to avoid becoming over overly reliant upon them. There needs to be a combination of approaches that integrate the benefits of each approach. For example, long-term goal setting to emphasise intrinsic motivation; individual, team, and whole class reward systems to boost extrinsic motivation; and praise utilised often enough to establish a positive learning environment.

Next, we are going to see how interaction patterns impact student engagement and learning.

Interaction patterns and engagement

Interaction patterns are the processes by which elements of a lesson, learners, and instructors interact. This section will give some insight into how this can support an online lesson.

The interaction patterns of a classroom are an instrumental aspect of proper student engagement online (Anderson, 2003). This is because certain interaction patterns enhance student engagement and stimulate student interest when learning online, such as learner to learner, learner to instructor and back, and learner to content (Bolliger & Martin, 2018). These interaction patterns assist students in their ability to achieve optimal educational outcomes (Chen et al., 2008). Think of learner to learner as students communicating together and of learner to instructor as interaction between student and teacher. Learner to content is where students are interacting with the learning materials through various formats, such as text, video, audio, interactive games, and online resources (Su et al., 2005).

Let's look at instructor perspectives and ways to implement and enhance these interaction patterns in your teaching practice.

Learner-to-learner interactions

Bolliger and Martin (2018) found that instructors valued learner to learner interaction enhancing activities in different ways:

- Over 90% valued icebreaker activities.
- Over 93% valued collaborative activities.
- Almost 90% valued interaction during student presentations.
- Over 80% valued peer review and peer assessments.

You can boost and enhance these interaction patterns in your classroom through the following types of activities:

- Having interactive introduction/icebreaker activities (Stepich & Ertmer, 2003) (see the context and warm-up sections in Chapter 11).
- Utilising break out rooms and having collaborative activities such as group research projects.
- Having students deliver presentations or asking whole class questions.
- Having students give feedback on each other's work.

Through these sorts of collaborative learning, a deeper sense of community is established, which can lead to deeper learning (Shackelford & Maxwell, 2012). Research on this topic also indicates that when student collaboration is increased, student satisfaction with the course also goes up (Jung et al., 2002).

Learner-to-instructor interactions

Bolliger and Martin (2018) found that instructors valued some learner-to-instructor, interaction-enhancing activities more than others:

- Over 95% rated regular announcements and email reminders.
- Over 90% consider an informal question and answer forum to be important or very important.

- Almost 90% rated using student names and posting grading rubrics highly.
- Over 80% rated using reflections.

It was also found that regular communication with learners via discussion, announcement, and email was considered most important.

You can boost and enhance these interaction patterns in your classroom through the following types of activities:

- Sending out regular announcements and updates to parents and students (where necessary).
- Making use of an informal teacher/family forum or blog.
- Utilising a live video platform so you can have live lessons with students and parents.
- Using the break out room function during independent work sessions to have more personalised 1-to-1 discussions with students.
- Sharing rubrics with students that are in student language.
- Either memorising student names or, if you have too many to remember, simply having students make name tags and have them on display (alternatively, find a live video platform that shows student names).

Through enhancing, tailoring, and building learner-to-instructor interactions in your classroom, it is more likely that student satisfaction and achievement will occur (Andersen et al., 2013).

Learner-to-content interactions

Bolliger and Martin (2018) found that instructors valued learner-to-content, interaction-enhancing activities in different ways:

- Over 94% considered structured discussions to be important or very important.
- Almost 94% think students should work on realistic scenarios.
- Over 92% think that content should be interacted within more than one media format.
- Reflecting on learning was rated highly by over 87% of instructors.

You can boost and enhance these interaction patterns in your classroom through the following types of activities:

- Utilising group discussions through break out rooms.
- Tackling real-world issues during projects.
- Using a few different platforms and even having students do some work in "off screen time." This can be done by using audio calls and having students work on independent projects, or by setting group work where they split up responsibilities.
- Having students complete post-class reflections to demonstrate what they found difficult and what they found easy.

Leaner-to-content interactions are critical as they enable students to engage with the instructional content, materials, and activities (Tuovinen, 2000).

Context, meaningful learning, and gamification?

I recently wrote an article for *Times Educational Supplement* where I delved into the details of why having relatable context is important for students. Basically, if all the learning seems pointless, all the drive to engage with learning materials needs to come from a reward system, which can be useful but does get old (Macur, 2020). This is even reflected in adults; teachers undergoing their teacher training have reported that meaningful learning is beneficial to their own learning and future teaching practice (Kostiainen et al., 2018). While it can be difficult to think of ways to make content meaningful and contextual, it can also be quite simple. We will look at some ways to do that.

Context and meaningful learning

Students need to connect with and understand why they are learning a topic, lesson, idea, concept, or even word (Macur, 2020). Through delivering countless online lessons, observing teachers doing this, and interviewing teachers for their own toolkits, a few key ways to do this stood out that can be easily applied to your online practice:

- Using real-world scenarios for students to solve problems (e.g. splitting a birthday cake to learn about pie charts).

- Using relatable cartoon characters in the lesson delivery.
- Using student names where appropriate in the content (e.g. when demonstrating story starter sentences, you could say "Once upon a time, Greg . . .").
- Linking learning goals to the reward system of the lesson (e.g. having teams with the keyword names).

This is somewhere that you can get creative and think of ways to present the content of the course in situations and scenarios that the students will be interested in and have some prior knowledge about.

Next, let's look at some key points about gamification.

Gamification

Gamification is often recognised as a great way to enhance student engagement and academic performance (Hung, 2017). Bringing it into online learning is often much simpler than one may think. Let's just look over some of the general rules that are worth considering when trying to gamify some of the learning in your online class.

- Keep the focus on the students.
- Don't try to pack in too much or start with very elaborate and complex games.
- Technology can support you, but it does not need to be the focus; learning can be gamified simply by using movement activities or action-based question answering.
- Data is important, but make sure that when you collect it (such as participation or correct answers), it is not misinterpreted.
- Remember, this is about play and having fun; keep it light and positive where possible.
- Review the games after they play them/create them; innovating can be fun, but do it with care.

(Hung, 2017)

Considering the implementation of gamification in online learning is a great way to enhance an online teaching practice while continuing to support your students' learning and engagement (Duggal & Singh, 2021). As such, this can be a core part of your planning and teaching methodology.

Conclusion

Having more engaging lessons reaps many benefits, including but not limited to improved academic performance and motivation (Trowler, 2010). As the online teacher for a class, it is important to focus on impacting engagement factors within your control, such as pace of lesson, difficulty of content, and levels of energy in the class. Equally, spending too much time and energy trying to impact things beyond your control, such as external noise, is not optimal.

Motivation and engagement are very closely related. Motivated students demonstrate characteristics such as willingness to participate, enthusiasm, and tenacity (Wentzel, 2020). As such, we should be aiming to build motivation in ways that work online. Typically, looking at intrinsically motivating things such as building students' thirst for knowledge and extrinsically motivational factors such as reward systems are helpful.

Student interaction patterns are also important; ensuring that students have a suitable amount of learner-to-learner, learner-to-instructor, and learner-to-content interactions helps to build a more effective online course/classroom (Bolliger & Martin, 2018).

Finally, providing students with meaningful and contextual learning helps keep them engaged and focused, as can the introduction of gamification if done correctly (Hung, 2017).

Key takeaways

- *Enhancing student engagement can positively impact student success, academic achievement, student satisfaction, student persistence, and social engagement (Trowler, 2010)*
- *Student engagement is the degree to which students are positively involved with the content, each other, the learning environment, and the instructor – as student engagement is optimised, learning goals are more easily met.*
- *Boring lessons, unmeaningful content, poor quality internet connection on the teacher's side, and pace of lesson are all areas in*

- which you as a teacher can impact student engagement quite easily (solutions in easy to influence section).
- Parents, external noise on the students' side, weather, distractions in the students' rooms, lack of student sleep, and student-side internet issues are areas that are difficult to impact (solutions in hard to influence section).
- Motivated students are positive, driven, goal oriented, tenacious, and stable (Wentzel, 2020).
- We can boost students' intrinsic motivation by encouraging collaborations (use break out rooms), focusing on positive reinforcement, having them set long-term goals, giving them choice, and showing genuine interest in students.
- We can boost extrinsic motivation by offering rewards, certificates, good grades, positive feedback, and reward systems (individual, team, and whole class).
- Utilising learner-to-learner, learner-to-instructor, and learner-to-content interaction patterns appropriately helps to foster an optimal learning environment (Bolliger & Martin, 2018).
    - This can be achieved using various educational tools/formats, such as text, video, audio, interactive games, and online resources (Su et al., 2005).
    - We can also make use of our educational platform functions, such as break out rooms, audio-only function, and blog functions to share updates.
- Using context and making learning materials relatable are great ways to keep students engaged. We can do this by using real-world scenarios, embedding popular cartoon characters in the presentation of materials, and including students in the content (where appropriate) (Macur, 2020).
- Gamification is another way to enhance engagement in the online classroom. However, keep the focus on the students, keep the games simple, use technology where appropriate, and update games/keep it fun (Hung, 2017).

Bibliography

Andersen, J. C., Lampley, J. H., & Good, D. W. (2013). Learner satisfaction in online learning: An analysis of the perceived impact of learner-social media and learner-instructor interaction. *Review of Higher Education and Self-Learning*, 81–96.

Anderson, T. (2003). Modes of interaction in distance education: Recent developments and research questions. In *Handbook of distance education* (129–144). Lawrence Erlbaum Associates Publishers.

Angelino, L. M., Williams, F. K., & Natvig, D. (2007). Strategies to engage online students and reduce attrition rates. *Journal of Educators Online*, 1–14.

Benabou, R., & Tirole, J. (2003). Intrinsic and extrinsic motivation. *The Review of Economic Studies*, 489–520.

Bolliger, D., & Martin, F. (2018). Engagement matters: Student perceptions on the importance of engagement strategies in the online learning environment. *Online Learning Journal*, 205–222.

Chen, P.-S. D., Gonyea, R., & Kuh, G. (2008). Learning at a distance: Engaged or not? *Journal of Online Education*, 4, 1–7.

Coates, H. (2007). A model of online and general campus-based student engagement. *Assessment and Evaluation in Higher Education*, 121–141.

Csikszentmihalyi, M. (2014). Intrinsic motivation and effective teaching. In M. Csikszentmihalyi (Ed.), *Applications of flow in human development and education* (pp. 173–187). Springer.

Duggal, K., & Singh, P. (2021). Intrinsic and extrinsic motivation for online teaching in COVID-19: Applications, issues, and solution. In F. Al-Turjman, A. Devi, & A. Nayyar (Eds.), *Emerging technologies for battling Covid-19* (pp. 327–349). Springer.

Fang, M., Gerhart, B., & Ledford Jr, G. E. (2013). Negative effects of extrinsic rewards on intrinsic motivation: More smoke than fire. *World at Work Quarterly*, 17–29.

HEFCE. (2008). *Tender for a study into student engagement*. Higher Education Funding Council for England.

Hu, S., & Kuh, G. (2001). Being (dis)engaged in educationally purposeful activities: The influences of student and institutional characteristics. In *The American educational research association annual conference* (pp. 10–14). Research in Higher Education.

Hung, A. C. (2017). A critique and defense of gamification. *Journal of Interactive Online Learning*, 57–72.

Jung, I., Choi, S., Lim, C., & Leem, J. (2002). Effects of different types of interaction on learning achievement, satisfaction and participation in web-based instruction. *Innovations in Education and Teaching International*, 153–162.

Kostiainen, E., Ukskoski, T., Ruohotie-Lyhty, M., Kauppinen, M., Kainulainen, J., & Mäkinen, T. (2018). Improving student teachers' digital pedagogy through meaningful learning activities. *Teaching and Teacher Education*, 71.

Krause, K., & Coates, H. (2008). Students' engagement in first-year university. *Assessment and Evaluation in Higher Education*, 493–505.

Macur, G. (2020, November 18). *Why we should take time to explain why topics matter*. Retrieved November 14, 2021, from Times educational supplement: www.tes.com/news/lesson-context-explain-why-learning-lesson-important

McLean, A. (2003). *The motivated school*. Sage.

Meyer, K. A. (2014). Student engagement in online learning: What works and why. *ASHE Higher Education Report*, 1–114.

Shackelford, J. L., & Maxwell, M. (2012). Contribution of learner to learner interaction. *International Review of Research in Open & Distance Learning*, 228–249.

Stepich, D. A., & Ertmer, P. A. (2003). Building community as a critical element of online course design. *Educational Technology*, 33–43.

Su, B., Bonk, C. J., Magjuka, R. J., Liu, X., & Lee, S. (2005). The importance of interaction in webbased education: A program-level case study of online MBA courses. *Journal of Interactive Online Learning*, 1–19.

Trowler, V. (2010). Student engagement literature review. *The Higher Education Academy*, 1–15.

Tuovinen, J. E. (2000). Multimedia distance education interactions. *Educational Media International*, 16–24.

Wentzel, K. R. (2020). *Motivating students to learn*. Routledge.

Wentzel, K. R., & Miele, D. (2016). *Handbook of motivation at school* (2nd ed.). Routledge.

Body language and instructions in the online classroom

I will never forget the first time I turned my camera upside down to re-engage a class of 5-year-old students, or when I started pinning actions to words and the students found it easier to remember them. Since then, I have seen that tiny alterations to body language make huge impacts on student experience and teacher feelings of self-efficacy. Not to mention how proper giving of instructions impacted my student engagement and task completion rates.

This chapter covers how teachers can use their gestures, cues, and body language to help in an online lesson. It also includes how actions can be used to support learning. Benefits of correct posture are covered, along with the positives of applying these ideas properly. Good practice for giving instructions is discussed and modelled; concepts like instruction checking questions are a part of this. The conclusion is that through the use of proper body language and giving concise instructions, teachers give students the best chance of accessing the curriculum.

Aims of the chapter

By the end of this chapter, you will know:

- *What are body language, gestures, and cues?*
- *How gestures, cues, and body language help in an online lesson and how to use them to solve common problems in your class.*
- *How to use correct posture and why it is both healthy and helpful.*

DOI: 10.4324/9781003250630-5

Body language and instructions

- *How to give instructions and tricks to support this in an online class.*
- *Methods of modelling and demonstrating tasks online.*

Done right vs. done wrong

The following are two scenarios of online classrooms. Scenario A is an example where the teacher uses poor body language and complex instructions that overload the students. Scenario B is an example where the teacher uses engaging and positive body language and gives instructions in a staged, structured, and simple manner. While you read these two examples, think about how you would feel if you were the teacher of either of these two classes.

Scenario A

Time for class: shoulders aching, back in pain, frown on face. Start the video call. The teacher is slouched down, with his head rested on a hand and an uncomfortable hunch in his back (looking particularly disengaged and bored). The students slowly start to imitate this, and the joy simply seeps out of them.

As the teacher greets the class, there are no smiles and very little movement, just a monotone voice and some microphone testing. The teacher says: "get a pencil and a piece of paper." There is very little movement; maybe the students are not listening, or maybe the microphone is not working. So, the teacher says it again, louder; one student gets some paper, and slowly others start to do the same. This takes far longer than it should.

The teacher then starts to give the students the instructions, using long, complex sentences, e.g. "first, take your pencil, put it on the paper and draw a straight line down what would be the middle of an eye, make sure it is not too thick or thin and then draw another line to show a plus sign." This is overwhelming enough, but just to top it off, all of the instructions are given at once, and the teacher then says begin. A lost and confused faces look at the teacher; nobody knows what they are supposed to do. Frustrated, the teacher says the instructions again. One or two students begin to do

Body language and instructions

something resembling the activity, while the rest just pretend they are doing something or simply get distracted by other things in their rooms.

Time drags on. Some students complete the task; at this point of the lesson, students are drained and bored, the teacher just wants it to end, and nobody has gained anything positive from this experience.

At the end of the lesson, the teacher, in a long-winded and confusing way, tells the students to show their work. Some of them get confused and say goodbye and leave the class, some of them show a blank sheet, and only one or two managed to do the task.

Everybody says goodbye and the class ends.

The teacher has to go and lay down due to backache. The students leave wondering why their teacher is so boring, and parents are not happy that their children absolutely do not like their online lessons.

Scenario B

Time for class – sat up straight, shoulders back, smile on face, the teacher begins the live chat. Some of the students follow suit, sitting up with good posture; for those who do not, the teacher says, "1, 2, 3, eyes on me," and the students say, "1, 2, eyes on you." Then the teacher lifts his hands and taps his shoulders; the students know this cue, and all sit in the correct manner.

Greetings are pinned with a smile, and the teacher holds up a flashcard with an image of a pencil and paper. The students grab their pencils and papers, fast and efficient.

The teacher explains, "Today, we will be learning to draw the eyes of a character. Point your cameras at your papers." The teacher moves their cameras to face their paper, and the students follow suit.

Instructions are given in small steps and supported by a model from the teacher, e.g. the teacher says, "First, we draw a line down the middle," and then demonstrates how this would look by drawing it on their own paper.

As the task is completed, the teacher moves his camera back to face himself and starts to tap his shoulders; students know this is the cue to show they are sitting properly and follow suit.

A showtime flashcard is shown and students start to raise their hands. The teacher picks them to stand up one by one and show their drawing to the class.

The class is over and the students all say goodbye, waving and smiling. The teacher gets a flurry of positive messages from the parents and is more than comfortable to have another class – no backache, no postural problems!

Body language and instructions

> *The two scenarios here are far too common. Many teachers, students, and professionals that spend a lot of time behind computers end up with back problems. Not to mention the demotivated and demoralised lessons/work environments that can stem from poor posture and a lack of engaging body language. It should also be apparent that throwing a collection of instructions at students while teaching online is not going to end well.*

Introduction

Body language is a fundamental aspect of communication in the classroom. This remains the same whether it is an online classroom or an in-person classroom. What do we mean when we say body language? Body language is the combination of movements, postures, gestures, and cues that we give using our body. It incorporates all aspects of how we use our body when communicating, whether this is the movement of our arms or simply the hunching and slumping of our shoulders. A good way to think of this is as nonverbal communication (Miller, 2005).

Gestures are movements that can indicate a meaning; sometimes these are also called TPR (total physical response) and are used to link the meaning of a word to more than just the sound. This has been shown to be an effective tool when working with language learning students (Bahtiar, 2017).

Cues, in this book, are going to be the movements that a teacher can make to indicate that the students need to do something. For instance, if students are all playing with things on their desks and the teacher puts their hands on their head, the students follow suit. In this example, the students needed to put the toys down; the cue the teacher used to stop this was touching their head, and as the students follow this, they have to put the things down. The teacher could follow up by simply requesting the students move the things they were playing with from the desk, to reduce the likelihood of this repeating.

This chapter will look at how these key concepts can support online learning and the online learning environment.

How gestures, cues, and body language help in an online lesson

It is quite well known that frequent, positive, and engaging nonverbal communication positively impacts the effectiveness of education and students' academic progress (Bambaeeroo & Shokrpour, 2017). That being said, in an online classroom, does it really matter?

Yes. Not one of the teachers I spoke to when doing research on the kinds of topics that need to be addressed in the online education world thought it was not an important aspect of online education. Some even put forward that is it one of the most important aspects. This is something I happen to agree with; if I were your teacher and you saw me hunched over, looking bored like the teacher in Scenario A, you would react the exact same way as the students.

Let's look at some practical ways to use your body language and nonverbal communication in your own teaching practice.

How to use body language, gestures, and cues to solve common problems in your class

Body language can resolve a range of issues that commonly appear in the classroom. When effectively used, it can turn an okay lesson into a great one (White & Gardner, 2013).

To some degree, you are going to think of your own ways to do this, however, so you have a toolkit ready for your classes, here is a list of common problems I have seen over the years, and methods that have positively impacted these problems.

Table 5.1 How body language, gestures, and cues can solve common problems in the online classroom

	Body language	Gestures	Cues
Misbehaviour	Sitting up straight and moving closer to the camera can reduce misbehaviour and draw attention back to the teacher.	Moving closer to the screen and putting a finger over the lips can stop unwanted talking.	Clapping a routine clap can get the students' attention and bring them back to the task.

(Continued)

Body language and instructions

Table 5.1 (Continued)

	Body language	Gestures	Cues
Bored students	Using bigger movements and smiling more.	Pull a funny face or turn your camera upside down; this has never failed to get a laugh and takes the edge off a difficult or complicated task.	Using a more fun clapping routine, slowly making it very fast, and having the students try to imitate it.
Tired students	Sitting up straight, avoiding yawning, smiling frequently, and moving around a lot can help this.	Again, funny actions, faces, or silly things with the camera can perk students back up.	Having a stand-up cue is useful to get the students standing and their blood flowing a bit more; sometimes boredom seeps in as a result of sitting down for too long.
Confused students	Avoiding hunching up and looking stressed; students need to know you are there to support them through the difficult concepts. Smile warmly and try again.	Use actions when teaching new words. Pinning an action to the word can help students remember the word. This is useful when concepts stack and students need to remember the meanings of words to understand a concept as a whole.	Have a movement that students can use to show they need help or that they don't understand. Make it an obvious one so you don't miss it, like putting a finger on their forehead.
Distracted students	Using bigger movements is effective at bringing their attention back to you.	Humour often works, As does having an action pinned to the fact that you are about to dish out some rewards. For instance, before you give out points for the teams, you could move the pen that you use to do this closer to the camera.	Using visible and audible attention grabbers such as clapping routines is a good go to.

Body language and instructions

As you can see, the tools can be quite easily applied to different scenarios; when you try them out, you will be shocked at how effective and impactful they are at resolving the problems that you face. It should also be noted that incorporating these into your teaching practice is relatively cost-free and time effective, and the range of benefits is extensive (White & Gardner, 2013).

Considering the health and postural problems people face when they are behind a laptop/computer for long periods of time, we are now going to look at correct posture and its benefits. Remember, you are a model for your students; if you don't get this right, you could be setting them up for a lifetime of problems.

How to use correct posture and why it is both healthy and helpful

A 2007 study looked at how students aged 9 sat while they worked at computers. It indicated that, on a scale of 1 to 4, 1 being acceptable seating and 4 needing immediate change, none of the students started by sitting in an acceptable way. Sixty percent were at number 2 on the scale, 38% were at number 3, and 2% were at number 4. As time went on, the postures of the students slowly devolved and became worse. Discomfort was found to be associated with the poor posture that the students were adopting (Breen et al., 2007). A study that followed the same model found shockingly similar results with 0% of students in level 1, 65% of students in level 2, 30% of students in level 3, and 5% of students in level 4 (Kelly et al., 2009). The long-term impacts of this can be minor, such as aches and pains, or they can be major, such as scoliosis, kyphosis, and lordosis (Quka, 2015).

What does this mean? Well, first of all, remember that as their teacher, you are a model for them to emulate to some degree. Also, you are not immune to these problems yourself; seated and sedentary jobs can lead to back pain and back problems (Burdorf et al., 1993). This being the case, it is important for you to know a pathway to correct posture and to inform your students and parents of this.

How to sit and set up your equipment

The National Health Service in the UK lists a breakdown of guidelines for sitting behind a computer in a healthy way. You can make a student-friendly

Body language and instructions

poster out of these and share it with students and parents, encouraging them to put them up on the wall near where they have their online classes. You can also have a lesson where you teach the students about this and they create their own proper posture poster.

1. Use an adjustable chair with back support – get a chair that has adjustable heights and set it up so that legs are at right angles and feet are placed comfortably on the floor. This reduces strain on the back.
2. Make sure the keyboard is at a level where the forearms can be parallel with the floor; this can reduce the chances of repetitive strain injury.
3. Avoid crossing your legs, as this can lead to postural problems.
4. Raise your screen to eye level – this can be done by using a monitor stand and is a good way to keep your head in the right position.
5. Keep the mouse close, rather than having to reach across the table and strain the shoulders. Do the same with regularly used objects (e.g. stapler).

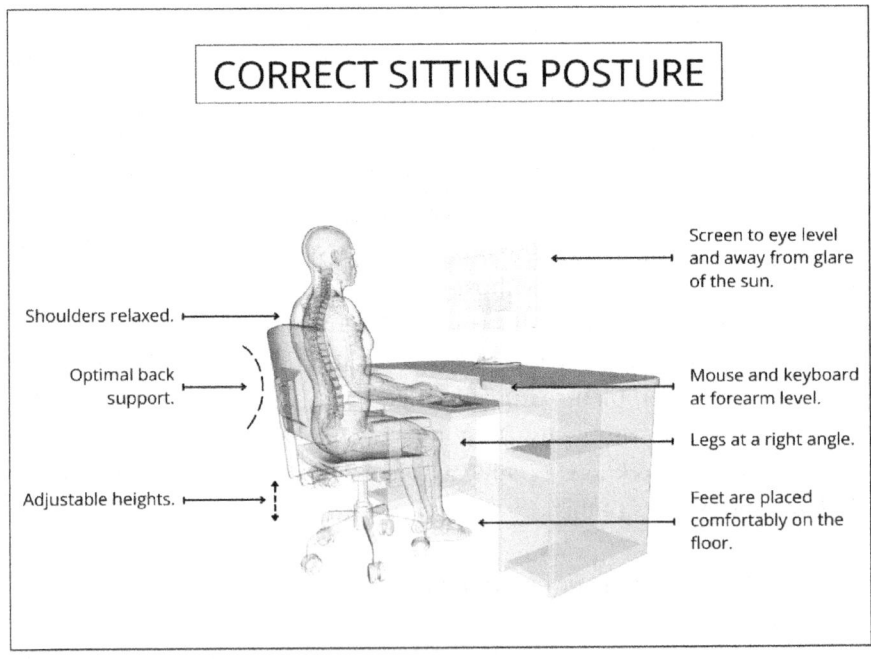

Figure 5.1 An example of proper sitting posture

6 Position your screen so that there is no glare from the sun or bright lights – you can also adjust the brightness so that it is not too intense on the eyes.
7 Take frequent breaks.

(NHS, 2019)

These may seem like small things, but they make a big difference. If you are in pain, you are distracted, and this can lead to misbehaviour along with student frustration, missed learning goals, low engagement, and, worst of all, long-term health problems for you and your students.

How to give instructions and tricks to support this in an online class

Instructions are what a teacher says and models to students with regard to what they need to do. Giving instructions effectively is essential to proper lesson progression and completion (Dean & Hubbell, 2012). Research has indicated that online teachers have not been prepared for online instructions (Chang & Fang, 2020). As such, this section is something that should really be considered deeply before starting your first online class.

Online teachers will need to give instructions at many different stages and for many different reasons during your class. These include (but are not limited to):

1 Setting rules.
2 Explaining activities.
3 Demonstrating/modelling activities.
4 Setting routines.
5 Setting teams and showing incentives.

In our online lessons, we need to give clear instructions during lessons; well-delivered instructions reap great rewards, such as focused students, completed tasks, motivated learners, met lesson objectives, fun and interactive classes, well timed classes, and much more. Poorly delivered instructions open the doors to a variety of problems, such as confused students, incomplete tasks, demotivated and demoralised students, boredom, misbehaviour, missed lesson objectives, and much more.

Body language and instructions

Think back to the two scenarios at the start of this chapter. The instructions given in the lesson that went poorly were complex and convoluted. This is ineffective. Here is an example of some instructions I observed in a highly effective teacher's lesson:

1. First, read the questions on your worksheet. (3 minutes)
2. Second, read the text on page 32 of your workbook; while reading, answer the questions on your worksheet. (10 minutes)
3. Third, once you have answered the questions on the worksheet, use your blue-tack to stick it to the wall, so we can see it on your camera. (2 minutes)
4. Fourth, look at other students' answers, and see if you came to the same conclusions. (5 minutes)
5. Finally, we will have a class discussion about the answers. (5 minutes)

The teacher first read the instructions and then left them up on a screen share. They gave reminders and used a timer for each section of the activity so students had a visual aid for their time limit.

Let's look at how instructions can knit into the establishment of classroom rules.

Ten instructional rules to remember

Amid the swath of research and literature surrounding the proper delivery of instructions, some of the best things I have come across are from the realms of bilingual and EAL instruction. This is because teachers in this context have to be extra careful so as not to confuse their students (since their students will not know a lot of words that fluent English speakers will). So, here are some great rules for you to think over as you give instructions (Sowell, 2017):

1. Plan your instructions before delivering them.
2. Keep instructions clear and concise.
3. Unless students need materials, do not get them to collect them before delivering the instructions (they may get distracted).
4. Use visual aids for your instructions if possible.
5. Use actions and images for commonly used instructions like "get a pencil."
6. Make sure you have the students' attention before starting – use one of your attention grabbers (a clapping routine or a movement cue).

7 Model and demonstrate your activities. This is far more effective than simply telling the students what to do.
8 For long sets of instructions, considering staging them and giving them one stage at a time, e.g.
   a Cut out the triangles, stick them to the circles, write your name on the back, and colour the front blue. – Too much info for young kids!
   b Cut out the triangles (wait for them to do this before moving on).
   c Stick them to the circles (wait for them to do this before moving on).
   d Write your name on the back (wait for them to do this before moving on).
   e Colour the front blue (wait for them to do this before moving on).
9 Use ICQs (instructional checking questions), e.g. if you say, "Use your red pencil," the ICQ could be: "Will you use the red pencil or the blue pencil?"
   a These give you the opportunity to check the students have understood what has been asked. This can also be done in a humorous way to engage students who may need extra stimulation during classes. They should be simple and are ideally "yes" or "no" questions.
10 Use CCQs (concept checking questions). For instance, if the students are building a water cycle project, you could ask them, "does the evaporation happen to the clouds or the water?"
   a These make sure that students understand the concepts they are navigating.

There are of course other things that may be relevant for you to consider, think of, and apply during your online practice; however, these ten key pointers will form a strong foundation for your delivery of instruction. A final point on the use of questions – as you ask these, they provide you key information as well as supporting the students growth; as such, be conscious of how students struggling with questions can mean they need additional support (Rosenshine, 2012).

Methods of modelling and demonstrating tasks online

Modelling an activity and demonstrating an activity are synonymous; it is important to know this, as these two words are used interchangeably by

Body language and instructions

many schools. Modelling an activity is typically where a teacher shows the students how to complete an activity or how a concept works or demonstrates a process (Chaucer School, n.d.). It is well known as a better method of guiding the students to completion of a task than simply giving them instructions/telling them what to do (Antonius et al., 2007).

To make things as straight-forward and digestible as possible, a list of the ways that teachers can model and demonstrate an activity in an online class is presented in Table 5.2.

While giving a model or a demonstration of what to do, make sure you consider the ten rules mentioned earlier, as they are still relevant and support the modelling process.

The next section will conclude the ideas that have been covered here and provide some semblance of recap.

Table 5.2 Methods of modelling and demonstrating in the online classroom

Method of modelling and demonstrating	How to do this in your online classroom
Using multimedia.	Play a pre-prepared video of what the students need to do on screen share; this can be sped up so that time is not wasted.
Showing the students step by step.	Guiding the students through the activity in a step-by-step manner is a very structured way to model; you can turn your camera and face it towards whatever project you are working on so the students can follow suit.
Showing a completed project.	If the students are creating something physical at home, say a rainforest showing its four layers, you could show them examples in the form of pictures or even one that you made earlier.
Demonstrating the concept in action.	This works well with new language, e.g. if the students were learning how to add an adjective to a sentence, you could use two images, one of a small car and one of a big car. You could point at the small car and say, "It is a small car." Then point at the big car and say, "It is a big car." This shows them what the concept looks like in action.
Demonstrating the process in action.	A good example of this would be water turning into steam. You could take your camera and show them a kettle boiling, showing them the water turning into steam.

Conclusion

Body language, gestures, and cues are nonverbal methods of communication (Miller, 2005). Using them correctly can reap a range of benefits, from positively impacting academic progress to increasing the effectiveness of the education process (Bambaeeroo & Shokrpour, 2017). Not one of the teachers spoken to when conducting research for this book thought these were trivial aspects of the online class. They can be used to clear up a range of issues that teachers face, including misbehaviour, bored students, tired students, confused students, and distracted students.

Posture is a key part of health consideration in the online classroom. Two studies showed that 0% of students sat in acceptable posture when they are starting an online lesson, and that as lessons progress, posture worsened (Bambaeeroo & Shokrpour, 2017; Kelly et al., 2009). This is a major issue as incorrect posture is associated with health risks in both the short term and the long term (Quka, 2015; Burdorf et al., 1993). As the class teacher, it is important to inform students of proper posture and equipment set up. It is also important to model this yourself, for both student benefit and your own health.

Giving instructions and modelling activities effectively is fundamental to the delivery and proper completion of a lesson (Dean & Hubbell, 2012). Instructions are given for a variety of reasons; some key times are: rules explaining activities, setting routines, and developing reward systems. When delivered correctly, students are more likely to be able to complete a task. To achieve this, they should be concise and clear. It is often a useful strategy to stage the instructions, showing the students them in a step-by-step manner. Using visual aids, planning instructions, and delivering them when students' attention is on the teacher are also advantageous (Sowell, 2017). Teachers can also utilise ICQs and CCQs to check students have understood the instructions and concepts. This is best done through simple "either/or" or "yes/no" questions.

Modelling alongside instruction is often the best approach to use, as it gives the students a clearer pathway and set of actions to follow (Antonius et al., 2007). This can be done in many ways, such as the use of multimedia, demonstrating a concept, showing the students step by step, and/or demonstrating a process are some examples of this.

Body language and instructions

As online teachers, we need to be diligent with regard to these key aspects of an online lesson; utilising these skills properly is a recipe for a successful online classroom.

Key takeaways

- *Body language, gestures, and cues are all nonverbal communication, including from how we sit, to how we move our arms and even our facial expressions (Miller, 2005).*
- *Frequently using engaging and positive nonverbal methods of communication is a good way to enhance your online teaching practice (Bambaeeroo & Shokrpour, 2017).*
- *The following exhibitions of body language, gestures, and cues can alleviate common problems that arise in educational contexts (White & Gardner, 2013):*
  - *Body language. Sitting up straight, using bigger movements, avoiding yawning or hunching, or looking stressed.*
  - *Gestures. Moving closer to the camera, putting a finger over your lips, pulling a funny face, turning your camera upside down using TPR.*
  - *Cue. Clapping routines, stand-up cues, sit-down cues, movement cues, support cues, and visual cues.*
- *Students do not naturally sit in an acceptable posture when they start an online lesson.*
  - *As a lesson goes on, their posture worsens (Bambaeeroo & Shokrpour, 2017; Kelly et al., 2009).*
  - *There are long-term and short-term health implications associated with poor posture such as aches, pains, lordosis, scoliosis, and kyphosis (Quka, 2015; Burdorf et al., 1993).*
- *As a teacher, it is our responsibility to model correct posture and how to set up a computer space so it alleviates the negative impacts of sitting behind a computer screen.*
  - *This can be done by using an adjustable chair, having legs at right angles with feet on the floor, having the elbows bent at*

> right angles, avoiding crossing legs, having the computer screen at eye level, avoiding hunching over, and keeping equipment close by (NHS, 2019). Make a student-friendly poster of this and send it to your students and parents so it can be put up on the wall in the study area.
> - *Instructions should be clear, concise, and planned. Delivery of instructions should be logical and scaffolded. Visual aids can be used (Sowell, 2017), and you can leave instructions up on your screen using screen share if needed.*
> - *When giving instructions, it is often more effective to give a model or demonstrate an activity (Antonius et al., 2007). This can be done by showing a completed project, demonstrating a concept, or even showing the students in a step-by-step manner – through the medium of screen share or by directing the camera to what you are doing.*

Bibliography

Antonius, S., Haines, C., Jensen, T. H., Niss, M., & Burkhardt, H. (2007). Classroom activities and the teacher. In *Modelling and applications in mathematics education* (pp. 295–308). Springer.

Bahtiar, Y. (2017). Using the total physical response to improve students' vocabulary mastery. *SELL Journal: Scope of English Language Teaching, Linguistics, and Literature*, 9–23.

Bambaeeroo, F., & Shokrpour, N. (2017). The impact of the teachers' non-verbal communication on success in teaching. *Journal of Advances in Medical Education & Professionalism*, 51–59.

Breen, R., Pyper, S., Rusk, Y., & Dockrell, S. (2007). An investigation of children's posture and discomfort during computer use. *Ergonomics*, 1582–1592.

Burdorf, A., Naaktgeboren, B., & de Groot, H. C. (1993). Occupational risk factors for low back pain among sedentary workers. *Journal of Occupational Medicine*, 1213–1220.

Chang, C. L., & Fang, M. (2020). E-learning and online instructions of higher education during the 2019 novel coronavirus diseases (COVID-19) epidemic. *Journal of Physics*, *1574*, 012166.

Chaucer School. (n.d.). *Effective modelling*. Retrieved December 1, 2021, from Chaucer School: www.chaucer.sheffield.sch.uk/images/schoolimprovement/tla/modelling.pdf

Dean, C. B., & Hubbell, E. R. (2012). *Classroom instruction that works: Research-based strategies for increasing student achievement*. ASCD.

Kelly, G., Dockrell, S., & Galvin, R. (2009). Computer use in school: Its effect on posture and discomfort in schoolchildren. *Work*, 321–328.

Miller, P. W. (2005). Body language in the classroom. *Techniques: Connecting Education and Careers*, 28–30.

NHS. (2019, 07 18). *How to sit at your desk correctly*. Retrieved November 30, 2021, from NHS: www.nhs.uk/live-well/healthy-body/how-to-sit-correctly/

Quka, N. S. (2015). Risk factors of poor posture in children and its prevalence. *Academic Journal of Interdisciplinary Studies*, 97–97.

Rosenshine, B. (2012). Principles of instruction: Research-based strategies that all teachers should know. *American Educator*, 12–39.

Sowell, J. (2017). Good instruction-giving in the second-language classroom. *English Teaching Forum*, 10–19.

White, J., & Gardner, J. (2013). *The classroom x-factor: The power of body language and non-verbal communication in teaching*. Routledge.

Working with parents online

I used to routinely have problems with parents complaining that I was not in contact enough. When I spoke to my line manager at the time, she told me something that totally changed everything. She advised that once a week, I should send a parent body email, addressing the parents of all my students saying how the lessons this week have been very enjoyable and that their children are wonderful humans. Within two weeks, I had parents messaging me saying how grateful they were that I was their child's teacher. Small changes like this make big impacts.

Parents are a big deal when teaching kindergarten and primary students. This chapter covers reasons why effective communication with parents is necessary and useful. It goes on the review effective methods of communication with parents. We then look into things that teachers can ask parents not to do, like whispering the answers to questions during lessons. Finally, we look at things that parents can do at home to support the online class. The conclusion is that parents can be a great resource for teachers, e.g. they can motivate their children and give them lots of positive reinforcement when they put in a good effort.

Aims of the chapter

By the end of this chapter, you will know:

- *What kind of concerns parents have about online education.*
- *The benefits that can be reaped from parent communication, interaction, and involvement.*

Working with parents online

- *Potential barriers/problems and how to overcome them.*
- *Effective ways to communicate with parents.*
- *Things parents should and shouldn't help with.*

Done right vs. done wrong

The following are two scenarios that demonstrate how two teachers of similar ability and calibre have very different experiences and results due to different approaches to parent communication. In Scenario A, the teacher only contacts parents when absolutely necessary and language use is not considered fully. In Scenario B, contact is established early, weekly updates are sent, and the language the teacher uses is carefully crafted so as to reduce the chances of overly negative reactions. Both teachers tell the truth, which is absolutely necessary; however, the results are wildly different.

Scenario A

Class starts in one week's time. Resources planned, materials ready, good; nothing to worry about till then.

First class delivered, good; no problems, students did well, formative assessments showed progress, some got distracted with toys but were put on task when the reward system was used.

Second class delivered, students improving, wonderful; no complaints from the teacher, none from the students. Distractions still continue but are easily resolved using engagement tactics.

A parent contacts the teacher to ask, "How is my son doing? Can you give some feedback on his progress?" The teacher responds: "Your son is doing fine. He is meeting the learning objectives."

Third class delivered, another good one, students did homework; three students did not show up, better email the parents. Engagement levels felt a little low, too; better think of a new reward system.

The teacher emails the three parents to say: "Tell your children that attending class is mandatory; they are at risk of getting behind in materials."

Fourth class delivered, two different students did not show up for class; better contact their parents and say the same.

Working with parents online

A flurry of emails come in, requesting feedback on student progress, complaining about lack of communication.

Fifth class, motivating students is becoming more difficult; many students did not show up, and as a result, many students are falling behind. Lateness and missed lessons are becoming a problem academically now. As is some parents telling students the answers during lessons.

Four parents contact the manager to complain the teacher for the class is not good; the academics are starting to reflect this and the students in the classroom look tired, bored, and distracted.

Sixth class today . . . a tired and dull look drifts across the teacher's face in the minutes before class. "Why are these students so unreliable and the parents so annoying?" thinks the teacher.

Scenario B

Class starts in one week's time. Resources planned, materials ready, good.

Time to email the parents reminding them of class times and some top tips about setting up the learning area for healthy posture and student engagement.

First class goes well, students on task, no distractions from toys or things in their learning space, all sitting nicely, and learning goals are met.

Time for a thank you email to the parents for setting up the students' learning spaces appropriately.

Second class is even better: students meet the learning goals and all score well on the end of class self-grading mini quiz that has been introduced, although some parents are whispering answers to them.

Time to send parents a guide on seeing the mini quiz results after each lesson. Some parents respond thanking the teacher for this. A request to not give students answers during lessons is phrased like this: "Please allow your wonderful children to make mistakes during lessons ☺ telling them answers can make me think they understand when they actually need a little more support."

Fourth class, all students present and on time; engagement levels have dropped for some reason, but learning goals are met.

Time for a parent instant messaging group notification asking parents to positively praise their children for the great lessons they are achieving, thus reinforcing the praise delivered in the classroom. Many parents show their support for this idea, praising the teacher for their hard work.

Fifth class, motivation levels are high; students are sat in a healthy manner and arrive on time for class. There are no distractions in their environment and class routines are well known.

Time to post clips and photos on the parent blog, showing the students engaging with the content, each other, and the instructor.

Each month, a parent feedback form is sent out. Parents are informed that this way they can feed back their thoughts and suggestions.

Sixth class is about to start. The teacher thinks: "These are some hard-working students, and their parents are so lovely!"

> *The two scenarios really do demonstrate how simple, regular, professional, and positive communication can improve the lessons you teach and make your life outside the classroom a lot easier. Miscommunication with parents is often the bane of a teacher's experience. However, I can attest that, when properly utilised, it is a positive tool that can be used in many productive ways.*

Introduction

It has been pointed out that in online education, the three main groups are students, teachers, and parents (Zhou & Li, 2020). On top of this, parent involvement in a child's online education has been reported by teachers and parents as having a big influence on academic achievement (Pek & Mee, 2020). As such, communicating with parents is an important and impacting aspect of a teacher's job. When this is done carefully and constructively, this relationship can lead to a range of positive impacts. However, when parent–teacher relationships go sour and/or communication is unclear/misleading, it can create problems for all involved (Dyches et al., 2011). But, how should communication happen? When should it happen? What tone should be used? Can teachers be very friendly with parents and treat them as buddies? These are great questions, and this chapter will cover them using research and practical guidance. Before we do that, let's look at some eye-opening statistics from around the world regarding parents and their thoughts, expectations, needs, and questions. While reading these, consider how failing to address these concerns could negatively impact the teacher–parent relationship.

China

A department of education survey in Heilongjiang, consisting of 1.28 million parent questionnaires, revealed that 92.33% of parents were very satisfied when schools and teachers were clear and regular in contact regarding the cautions and arrangements for online learning (Department of Education of Heilongjiang, 2020). What does this indicate? What could be taken from this statistic? One thing that can be drawn from it is that pretty much everybody knows that systems are not perfect, that there will be problems and challenges, that there will be issues that need to be overcome. What matters to people, specifically parents, is that they know about the problems, understand what challenges may arise, and receive some advice on overcoming the issues that will emerge.

A nationwide study in China revealed 40.9% of parents were worried about poor learning effectiveness (Wang et al., 2020). A survey of almost 10,000 parents of elementary parents in Sichuan demonstrated parent concerns regarding concentration (44.48%) and obscure learning times (44.06%). Further surveys indicated 52.4% of parents reported unfamiliarity with the online learning technologies and there were no effective solutions to problems they face; there were also concerns about eye health and a range of wellbeing-related factors (Zhou & Li, 2020).

India

A survey of 289 guardians in India brought forward some very alarming statistics: 81.7% reported online classes were less comfortable and 78.5% reported that they were less satisfactory. It was also found that 80.6% expressed children had poor attention in the online classroom, and 82.4% felt learning of subject theory and practice was lower. A range of distractions were reported, including online games, competitions, and surfing of the internet. Forty-five percent even reported a reduction in self-hygiene/care (Grover et al., 2021). Not all of these statistics can necessarily be put at the feet of online education, as the problems could be arising from a number of areas. However, these are concerns that parents have; as educators, it is our responsibility to consider and communicate ways to support parents to deal with these.

The UK and the US

A UK survey indicated that there are parental concerns regarding student support, learning quality, students viewing inappropriate materials, ethical inclusion of all in the class, and access in poorer areas of the country. This survey also indicated that there are reasonably significant differences in parent and child computer ability across the country (Livingstone & Bober, 2004), meaning that many parents will be ready to support their child in their set up of and exposure to online learning, while many will not have the skillset to do this.

A US survey consisting of 1290 parents indicated that parents report concerns that online education presents more risks for social emotional and mental health than in-person education. Also, that the online education approach may negatively impact health-supporting behaviours such as frequency of outdoor activity (Verlenden et al., 2021). Linking this to the Heilongjiang study, perhaps informing parents properly can alleviate the implications of this problem.

Why list all of these?

All of these problems and concerns that parents are reporting remain largely consistent globally. Whether parents are in the UK, the US, India, China, or any of the other places around the world, they routinely worry about students being able to access materials, technical problems, how to support their children, lesson quality, teacher quality, school communication, and wellbeing. How can we ease these concerns? The first survey mentioned in this chapter, the Heilongjiang study, gave us the answer. Almost all of the parents were satisfied if the teacher communicated with them.

So, communication is key, to use an old adage. As such, following a logical progression, next we will look at the benefits that can be reaped from parent communication, interaction, and involvement.

The benefits that can be reaped from parent communication, interaction, and involvement

Parent and family involvement can be a deeply helpful and supportive thing for teachers (Ntekane, 2018). There is an extensive literature that outlines and demonstrates the benefits, positive experiences, and outcomes that students experience as a result of strong teacher–parent relationships (Yazdani et al., 2020).

I have never interviewed for a teaching or leadership position that has not asked me about how I communicate and deal with parents. They are a vital asset that, when well-managed, supports students, teachers, and schools.

Some of the many benefits of proper parent–teacher working relationships/parental and guardian involvement are:

1   Enhanced student performance.
2   Reduction of absenteeism.
3   Increased parental belief in children's education.
4   Higher attainment with regard to grades.
5   Improved social skills.
6   Improved behaviour.

(Garcia & Thornton, 2014)

These ideas are backed up by(Lau et al. (2011), who put forward that the involvement of parents is associated with the following positive outcomes: academic outcomes, positive learning attitudes, and social emotional skills. The strength or weakness of the relationship has also been found to positively or negatively relate to reading and math performance (Yazdaniet al., 2020).

These key benefits stood out to all of the teachers who were interviewed in the process of preparing this book. You can also tell when a teacher has been routinely in touch with parents; key giveaways are that when observing their lesson, most of the students have not got toys and distractions in front of them. Also, some of them will have their computers set up to eye level and start the class sat with correct posture.

Potential barriers/problems and overcoming them

Considering the benefits of parent involvement is a wonderful idea; research has supported it as beneficial, and it has supported me personally a great deal. That being said, it must be done carefully and clearly. It is also true that a great number of issues can arise if done poorly. Some key ones are that it can negatively impact school achievement, cause disruptions to family life, and lead to problems, difficulties, and issues for teachers and school leaders (Lareau, 2019).

Relations between parents and teachers can deteriorate for a number of reasons. Some noted in the literature can be seen in Table 6.1.

Table 6.1 Potential barriers and problems while working with parents – and how to overcome them

Potential barriers and problems	Overcoming them
Parents constantly calling teachers to check on their children – which can lead to learners feeling untrusted by their parents (Llamas & Tuazon, 2016).	Have a weekly update email that you send out to the parent body confirming some basic details. You can also use a register app that notifies parents of attendance or lack of attendance. Be consistent.
Communication becoming a drain on the teacher's time (Epstein & Becker, 1982).	Have specific procedures that need to be followed, e.g. email hours, a 48-hour response window and a "calls for emergencies" policy. Weekly bulletins also reduce the FAQs that parents may have for you.
Miscommunication.	Put things in simple terms, give clear deadlines, and don't use students to pass on messages – send an email or a parent body update. You can use a class blog, too, but some parents will not check this.
Lack of communication.	This is a difficult one to deal with. Sometimes, sending positive news will get the quieter parents to respond.
Impact on student attitudes (Lasater, 2016).	Communicate to parents that students can be very impressionable, so to maximise their self-efficacy, as teachers and parents, we should offer praise and point out their strengths. That over-focus on development areas both at home and in school can give them a distorted sense of competence.
Inability or failed resolution of conflicts (Lasater, 2016).	Resolving conflicts can be challenging; overall, using positive language, responding not based on emotion, and trying to have a video call instead of an email stream can help.
Challenging parents (Lasater, 2016).	There are always challenging parents who perhaps need more support, information, or are simply more demanding. Have solid communication and feedback dates planned and informed ahead of time.

Potential barriers and problems	Overcoming them
Your own potential lack of training/ knowledge to deal with the problem (Lasater, 2016).	Here is a key failing for all of us: nobody is prepared to deal with all problems. The best way to address this is to speak to more senior teachers. If you do not know any, look online for articles on the specific problem; you will find one. See how other people have solved the problems and adapt their solutions for your situation.

There are, of course, many other problems that could arise; these are just some of the more common ones and some potential solutions that have worked for teachers in the past. One of the best ways to deal with problems is to solve them before they occur. The next section will introduce effective ways to communicate with parents. Do this well, and the frequency at which the problems you face arise will be reduced.

Effective ways to communicate with parents

We know what parents are concerned about, we know the benefits of proper parent communication methods, and we know some of the problems that can occur and how to overcome them. It is time to see some of the methods of communication that you can incorporate into your teaching practice, when they can take place, and why they are useful.

The use of multiple channels has been shown to be effective (Xia, 2020); some great ones to use are:

1   Instant message groups (IM groups).
    a   These are a great way of feeding back information in real time to parents. A word of warning – establish a rule that these are for announcements only; parents should communicate in a separate group, and if they have a question for you, they should follow the email process.
2   Class blogs.
    a   These are an effective way of sharing weekly updates, student work, images, and videos of students in classes (as long as they are in line with your safeguarding policy/parental consent is given).

3   Emails.
    a   Another good way to share weekly bulletins, updates, messages of positivity, and formal communication with parents on an individual basis.
4   A live register.
    a   This allows parents who are not able to be present to see student attendance to get either an email notification or to see a register after it has been taken.
5   Quiz websites.
    a   Parents will constantly be asking for student progress feedback. Giving a mini quiz at the end of each lesson allows parents to see how their children are performing and retaining the information. You can simply share a link to the results each week.
6   A shared drive.
    a   Share drives can be a good way to distribute large files that do not fit into an email. They are also a good place for students to submit pieces of work.
7   Microsoft forms.
    a   You can send out a monthly Microsoft forms document that allows parents to feed back their thoughts and feelings. This is a double win. Firstly, it stops anger building up and allows parents to vent if they have concerns. Secondly, it gives you an indication of where you may be missing the mark.
8   Phone calls/video calls.
    a   These are a good way to have a more personal conversation, especially if there is a complaint or problem. Parents are less likely to be confrontational if they speak to you instead of writing to you.

Using these platforms/methods of communication to monitor student progress and collect student homework/deliver student home learning is generally effective (Xia, 2020). It can also help to create the efficient and effective communication process we desire in order to enhance parent support and cooperation (Cheng, 2020).

Wonderful – now we have practical tools we can use for communication. Remember, if you have other ideas or methods of communication, try them out. This list is not exclusive.

Things parents should and shouldn't help with

There are many ways in which parents can support the learning of their children at home. As discussed, properly applied and communicated parental involvement improves a multiplicity of success factors (Ntekane, 2018). We also know that their involvement can cause more trouble than good if done incorrectly and without care, attention, or consideration (Lareau, 2019). We also have some good tools to communicate with parents. These things considered, let's look at what parents typically should be able to support and help with, and what they typically shouldn't be asked to help with. Please do consider, students are individuals, and perhaps in some contexts and/or scenarios, the following suggestions are not optimal. Judge this on a case-by-case basis.

Things to ask parents' support with

Research has indicated that around 20% of lesson time is wasted during online lessons due to students finding distraction and viewing other sites (McCoy, 2016). It was also demonstrated by an analysis that some methods of parental involvement are more effective than others, e.g. joint readings and discussions (Tan, 2020). As such, there are some areas in which calling upon parents for support is a good idea, and some where it is not. Here are nine easy suggestions that you can call upon when asking parents to support:

1. Praising their children for good work.
2. Setting up the learning area so it is not rife with distraction.
3. Setting up the learning area so the student sits healthily.
4. Reminding children of class times.
5. Giving rewards for improved behaviour and/or performance.
6. Sitting in lessons to help keep student focused.
7. Having discussions about what was learnt in class.
8. Joint reading of related materials to the class.
9. Creation of a timetable and/or schedule.

There are other ways in which parents can support you; this list is just a start and should only form some of the foundations of how you work together with parents. Now, let's look at things that you should avoid asking parents for support with.

Working with parents online

Things to avoid asking parents' support with

There are some things that parents might do off their own back, or that you might be tempted to ask for support with. Generally speaking, whenever I have seen teachers do these things, they tend to go poorly. Some of them to remember are:

1 Avoid asking parents to teach their children a concept (it can lead to negative parent–child interactions and misunderstood concepts).
2 Avoid asking parents for negative consequences for actions. When and if you need to involve parents in a consequences process, make it a positive/reflective process with a target or reward for improvement.
3 Parents will sometimes whisper answers to students during classes. Sometimes you won't even be able to hear it (mention this in your weekly updates, requesting parents avoid it and explaining that it can mislead you as a teacher, causing you to reduce support for that student when actually they need more).
4 Parents will sometimes do their children's homework (detrimental for the same reasons as above, resolved the same way).

These are the main four areas that I have seen causing issues for teachers during their online teaching practice. There are certainly more, and it is important to remain diligent and attentive to the communication processes and parent support process.

The next section will wrap up these ideas in a conclusion. This is a good opportunity to think about how these key ideas come together and create a concept that is "dealing with parents."

Conclusion

Around the world, parents are largely concerned with similar issues, such as poor learning effectiveness, wellbeing, and academic performance (Wang et al., 2020; Grover et al., 2021; Livingstone & Bober, 2004). However, almost all parents are satisfied if concerns and issues are shared and open communication is provided (Department of Education of Heilongjiang, 2020).

Parent and/or guardian involvement with the education process can be deeply beneficial if done carefully (Ntekane, 2018). Some of the many benefits include enhanced student performance, reduction of absenteeism, increased parental belief in children's education, higher attainment with regard to grades, improved social skills, and improved behaviour (Garcia & Thornton, 2014). That being said, it can also be a negatively impacting process that creates more issues and stresses than it resolves (Lareau, 2019). Overcoming these issues can stem from consistent and clear communication, establishing guidelines for teacher contact, using simple terms in communication, being positive in your approach to communication, and seeking advice from more senior teachers/online for problems you are unsure of how to solve.

Among the range of methods of communication available, using a selection can prove useful (Xia, 2020). Some options we talked about are: IM groups, class blogs, emails, live registers, quiz websites, a shared drive, Microsoft forms, and phone calls.

It is also worth noting that there are some things that parents should be asked to support with, and some things they should not. Overall, praise, reading, discussion, organisation, and learning space set-up are worth communicating to parents and requesting support for. Teaching concepts and applying negative consequences are some key areas in which you should avoid asking parents for help. It can also be communicated that completing the students' homework or providing answers during lessons is detrimental.

Key takeaways

- *Parental communication and involvement has both positive potential (Ntekane, 2018; Garcia & Thornton, 2014; Lau et al., 2011) and negative potential (Lareau, 2019).*
- *Regarding online education, parents are routinely concerned with education quality, student wellbeing, and academic performance (Wang et al., 2020; Grover et al., 2021; Livingstone & Bober, 2004).*
- *Communicating the problems that arise alleviates concerns from most parents; they want to be in the loop and prepared (Department of Education of Heilongjiang, 2020).*
- *A range of benefits can be reaped from parent communication; these impact academic performance, motivation, social skills and behaviour, and more (Garcia & Thornton, 2014).*

- *There are some potential barriers and problems that may arise; these include over-contact (Epstein & Becker, 1982), over-checking up on students (Llamas & Tuazon, 2016), parent impact on student attitudes, unresolved conflict, challenging parents, and poor teacher preparedness (Lasater, 2016).*
- *You can solve these barriers and problems by having communication procedures in place, using live feedback apps for registers/quizzes, putting things in simple terms, having consistent communication, being positive and professional in your communications, using multiple methods of communication, and seeking advice from more experienced teachers.*
- *The following are some key methods of communication that can be used: IM groups, class blogs, emails, live registers, quiz websites, a shared drive, Microsoft forms, and phone calls.*
  - *Using live feedback apps and websites such as quiz sites or registers reduces the need for parents to contact you to see if their child attended class and to check their performance.*
- *Some things to ask parents for support with are praise, reading, discussion, organisation, and learning space set-up.*
- *Some things to avoid asking for support with are teaching concepts and applying negative consequences.*

Bibliography

Cheng, X. (2020). Challenges of "School's Out, but Class's On" to school education: Practical exploration of Chinese schools during the COVID-19 pandemic. *Science Insights Education Frontiers*, 501–516.

Department of Education of Heilongjiang. (2020). *Big data analysis of 1.28 million questionnaires to explain the online teaching management of our province's basic education during the epidemic.* Retrieved December 4, 2021, from https://mp.weixin.qq.com/s/H6pxXH6pLc0uOqdUsJ9RIA.

Dyches, T. T., Carter, N. J., & Prater, M. A. (2011). *A teacher's guide to communicating with parents: Practical strategies for developing successful relationships.* Pearson Higher Ed.

Epstein, J. L., & Becker, H. J. (1982). Teachers' reported practices of parent involvement: Problems and possibilities. *The Elementary School Journal*, 103–113.

Garcia, L., & Thornton, O. (2014). The enduring importance of parental involvement. *NEA Today*.

Grover, S., Goyal, S. K., Mehra, A., Sahoo, S., & Goyal, S. (2021). A survey of parents of children attending the online classes during the ongoing COVID-19 pandemic. *The Indian Journal of Pediatrics*, 280–280.

Lareau, A. (2019). Parent involvement in schooling: A dissenting view. In C. L. Fagnano & B. Z. Werber (Eds.), *School, family and community interaction* (pp. 61–73). Routledge.

Lasater, K. (2016). Parent–teacher conflict related to student abilities: The impact on students and the family-school partnership. *School Community Journal*, 237–262.

Lau, E. Y., Li, H., & Rao, N. (2011). Parental involvement and children's readiness for school in China. *Educational Research*, 95–113.

Livingstone, S., & Bober, M. (2004). *UK children go online: Surveying the experiences of young people and their parents*. London LSE Research Online.

Llamas, A., & Tuazon, A. P. (2016). School practices in parental involvement, its expected results and barriers in public secondary schools. *International Journal of Educational Science and Research*, 69–78.

McCoy, B. R. (2016). Digital distractions in the classroom phase II: Student classroom use of digital devices for non-class related purposes. *Journal of Media Education*, 5–32.

Ntekane, A. (2018). *Parental involvement in education*. Retrieved December 4, 2021, from Research Gate: www.researchgate.net/profile/Abie-Ntekane/publication/324497851_PARENTAL_INVOLVEMENT_IN_EDUCATION/links/5ad09062aca2723a33472c9f/PARENTAL-INVOLVEMENT-IN-EDUCATION.pdf

Pek, L. S., & Mee, R. W. (2020). Parental involvement on child's education at home during school lockdown. *Journal of Humanities and Social Studies*, 192–196.

Tan, C. Y. (2020). Academic benefits from parental involvement are stratified by parental socioeconomic status: A meta-analysis. *Parenting*, 241–287.

Verlenden, J. V., Pampati, S., Rasberry, C. N., Liddon, N., Hertz, M., Kilmer, G., et al. (2021). *Association of children's mode of school instruction with child and parent experiences and well-being during the COVID-19 pandemic*. Morbidity and Mortality Weekly Report – CDC.

Wang, D., Wang, H., & Zhang, W. (2020). Research on online teaching during the pandemic of "School is Out, but Class is On": Based on a nationwide survey of 33240 online questionnaires. *Modern Educational Technology*, 12–18.

Xia, J. (2020). Practical exploration of school-family cooperative education during the COVID-19 epidemic: A case study of Zhenjiang Experimental School in Jiangsu province. *Best Evidence in Chinese Education*, 451–467.

Yazdani, N., Siedlecki, K. L., Cao, Z., & Cham, H. (2020). Longitudinal impact of sociocultural factors and parent beliefs on parent–teacher relationship strength. *The Elementary School Journal*, 1–33.

Zhou, L., & Li, F. (2020). A review of the largest online teaching in China for elementary and middle school students during the COVID-19 pandemic. *Best Evidence in Chinese Education*, 549–567.

Big classes, small classes, and 1-to-1

Having taught online to a wide range of class sizes, and having spoken to teachers about these three groups, similarities and differences have become apparent. I spoke to a teacher a few months ago who said teaching a large class was easier than a small class. Surprising, I know. The reasoning – and it is good reasoning because I have thought something similar before – was "small classes cover more content, so you have to plan a lot more." A true statement (fast finisher extensions are a good way to deal with that, by the way).

This chapter covers how to deal with differences in class sizes. Some teachers will be working in less affluent countries where the class sizes are 60–100 students wide. Some will be in countries like England, teaching class sizes in the 30s. Some will be in international schools with 14 and some will even have 1-to-1 classes. Throughout this chapter, we will explore the positives and challenges of each of these class sizes, and how to move past the challenges effectively. The conclusion is that while the class size differs, the fundamentals remain at least somewhat constant; with the correct tools at your disposal, you can navigate all three of these circumstances.

Aims of the chapter

By the end of this chapter, you will know:

- Some of the features of these class types.
- How to overcome the challenges of teaching big classes.

DOI: 10.4324/9781003250630-7

- *How to overcome the challenges of teaching small classes.*
- *How to overcome the challenges of teaching 1-to-1.*

Done right vs. done wrong

The following are two scenarios where a teacher has to navigate between the three types of classes. In both of these scenarios, the teachers use the same lesson format of: video input – discussion – reading – creative activity. However, Scenario A tries to deliver this format in the same way to each of the different class sizes. Scenario B delivers the same class but makes slight alterations to suit the class size. The results are quite different and highlight the importance of understanding how class size can impact lessons and what could/should be done. As you read these, think about how you might adapt to differing class sizes.

Scenario A

One-to-one class begins with the teacher introducing the topic using screen share and a multimedia video. At one point, the concentration wavers; the teacher says their name, and the student is present again. After this, a discussion is held; questions are asked that relate to the topic, and the student answers quickly and efficiently. Next comes a reading task; the student has a long paragraph to read on the screen and then must summarise it into two lines. Then, the student needs to create their own piece of text based on this idea – another task completed quickly. All materials are delivered, but there are still 10 minutes of class left. The teacher asks a stream of questions in a somewhat uncoordinated manner till the class is over.

Small class begins for 14 students; as the students arrive, a similar lesson structure is used. Saying student names to make them focus during the introduction video kind of works but is a little tedious. The discussion questions are asked individually, too; again, this kind of works but leaves many of the students sitting idly by. The reading task also faces some problems: many of the students complete it quickly, leaving them bored and slowly disengaging. The final creative task seems to go well, but many of the students appear drained and demotivated. As the last student finishes, the class ends.

Big classes, small classes, and 1-to-1

Big class begins for 50 students; during the video, at least half the class is not paying attention. The teacher repeatedly says names, but there are too many. During the discussion, most of the students do not get a chance to answer a teacher question; this causes them to turn off and not pay attention. Time is wasted. The reading task goes from bad to worse; five students complete it in 2 minutes, forty are still working, and five simply do not know what to do. This takes the rest of the lesson to navigate and the teacher does not finish the content.

Scenario B

One-to-one class starts and the video is played. At certain points in time, it is paused and open-ended questions relating to it are asked. Once it is finished, the teacher and student have a discussion about it. After that, the reading task is set and the student completes it quickly. The creative task is also completed quickly, too. Once it is completed, the teacher plays a pre-prepared review game till the end of class.

Small class starts. The video is played and paused; students are asked simple yes or no questions about the video and are rewarded individually for participating. The discussion is held in break out rooms and supported by questions provided by the teacher. During the reading task, there is an extension to attempt to turn the two lines into one line and then the one line into one word. The creative task also has an extension; the students are asked to reduce their own piece of text to two lines and then one. Class finishes on time.

Big class begins and the video is played. Students are asked simple yes or no questions relating to the content; they need to stand up for yes and sit down for no. The whole class is given a reward at the end if they participate. The discussion is also delivered in a plenary style, utilising the same game of stand-up sit-down. There are two separate reading options – a longer, more complex one and a shorter, simpler one. Students are asked to summarise them in the same way as the small class, starting with the fast one and then trying the challenge if they have time. The creative task has the same extension as the small class, and if both tasks are completed, the students can write a three-line reflection on what they learnt.

> *The two scenarios here really reflect how, as the class size grows, different strategies become an option/positive and potential learning tool. On the other hand, some things become more of a problem, require prior planning to navigate, and need different approaches; otherwise, lesson quality reduces.*

Introduction

Class size is a hot topic in the online education realm. Understanding that the class size can impact a range of important factors, such as student learning, pedagogical requirements, and financial returns, as well as the workload of the faculty involved, is essential (Taft et al., 2019).

It is said that there are three modes of teaching online education: delivering content to either small, large, or 1-to-1 classes (Lu, 2020). In reality, there are a multiplicity of ways to teach classes; these are just three ways to easily categorise class sizes. As such, these are the three that we will look at in a bit more detail, so that as a teacher, you are prepared and know what kind of tools you can bring into your online toolkit when approaching these. It is worth noting that even if you may only be tutoring or only teaching full class sizes. It is also worth reading up and learning about all three; you never know when you might be called upon to cover for or to take over a class that needs your support.

A study yielding 58 recent articles in academic journals indicated a few general themes. Firstly, larger classes work well for the learning of foundational and factual knowledge, as this requires less individualised teacher–student interaction. Small classes were found to be effective at delivering high order thinking skills, complex knowledge mastery, and development of skills. This being the case, there is no one size fits all (Taft et al., 2019). However, there are ways to enhance the way in which you deliver your classes whether they are large or small. There are ways to take advantage of the positives of the class size and alleviate the negatives. That is what we are going to be looking at.

How to overcome the challenges of teaching big classes

Typically, a larger class results in low levels of student engagement, poor student performance, and minimal opportunities to develop and practice skills such as critical thinking (Ehrenberg et al., 2001; McKeachie, 1980; Mulryan-Kyne, 2010). When working in an online environment, these conditions can potentially be compounded, especially if pedagogy that develops and utilises passive learning is utilised, or opportunity for direct contact with students is not properly adopted (Hornsby, 2020). A large class also usually results in a lack of or at least a lower amount instructor–student interaction (Lu, 2020), which, as we discussed in Chapter 4, is fundamental to the optimal running of online lessons.

These problems need to be navigated. Some of the ways to mitigate them, and/or to simply enhance your online teaching practice with large classes, are:

1 Make use of technology that supports learners at scale (Pishchukhina & Allen, 2021). There are websites, apps, and even platforms that help with this. The ones we mention in Chapter 2 are great at supporting all class sizes.
2 Frequent use of online quizzes has been fed back positively upon by students in surveys (Pishchukhina & Allen, 2021). These are very easy to use and, if done correctly, can self-grade instantly.
    a These also were related to sustained student engagement and students with the highest number of attempts at these quizzes correlated with improved performance in final results (Pishchukhina & Allen, 2021).
3 Make use of active learning. Just because the online classroom typically depicts students and teachers sat behind desks, it does not mean that you can incorporate some movement into the lessons (Hornsby, 2020). See Chapter 11 for ideas.
4 Equity and inclusion are essential. Bear in mind that students in your class may be from different cultures and even time zones; make assessments that allow all students to participate (Hornsby, 2020). See Chapter 9 for ideas.
5 Routine use of plenary questions and CCQs has stood out as useful over the online lessons I have observed, as is the use of break out rooms for

student collaboration. This is also reflected in a recent study (Hendarwati et al., 2021).

Ultimately, there are a multiplicity of challenges that you will face when navigating the teaching of large classes. Focus on getting students engaged and learning actively; passive learning behind a computer screen is a recipe for boredom and disengagement.

A top tip that I learnt the hard way is to avoid frequent change with large classes – there are so many students that sticking to the routines is essential.

How to overcome the challenges of teaching small classes

One major difference between larger classes and smaller classes is the amount of instructor to student interaction (Lu, 2020). Equally, students have more opportunities to participate simply by the rule of "splitting the pie." The fewer individuals there are to split between, the larger the share per person. That does not mean there are no challenges when teaching small classes. Some common ones are: content is moved through faster than expected, students still may become disengaged, students are more likely to get distracted by each other, and parent expectations may be higher.

Again, these problems need to be navigated and resolved, and they can be. Some key ways to teach a smaller class successfully are:

1. Plan extension activities to ensure there are materials ready should the class finish early. These should be planned carefully to ensure their effectiveness (Seymour-East, 2017).
   a. These can take the form of an additional task to complete or an extension for the activity being delivered.
2. Ensure students are not kept in their seats; take advantage of active learning and avoid excessive use of passive teacher-led instruction (Hornsby, 2020).
   a. This is a great strategy for all class sizes.
3. Take advantage of self-marking quiz platforms for providing performance feedback to parents (see Chapter 2 for more information). This (as demonstrated in Chapter 6) will also reap a whole range of other benefits.

4   Do some whole class projects, like a whole class presentation.
    a   I saw a great project-based learning presentation aimed at developing students' knowledge about the Renaissance period that was done as a whole class project. The students each had to prepare two slides lasting 1 minute in total, covering a progressing period of time. The teacher screen shared the PPT once the students had finalised it and did the slide movement as the class took turns.

Overall, there are many pros to smaller classes but, I would say, the planning process is longer, and unless you take advantage of the useful platforms available, the amount of feedback expected based on the number of students will be a monster of its own.

A top tip I learnt the hard way is that just because the class is small, it does not mean that break out rooms are not worth using. Even if you only have four students, you can make pairs. Take full advantage of the tools at your disposal.

How to overcome the challenges of teaching 1-to-1

Overall, a 1-to-1 tutoring class is known for creating personalised learning experiences. They also excel at maximising instructor to student and student to instructor interactions (Lu, 2020). This being said, historically, a multiplicity of research has shown that tutoring has been very successful in some cases, and apparently non-impacting in others (Shanahan, 1998). This is more recently mirrored in studies that indicated that while students felt positively about their online tutoring experiences, it was not clear whether this impacted their academic performance (Offenholley, 2014; Zhang, 2013).

So, while the 1-to-1 class may seem like it is the crème de la crème, it clearly faces its own challenges. Some of these that stood out to me and have been reported by Cambridge University Press are: lack of student opportunity for student–student interactions; excess amount of student–instructor interaction; often a lack of other teachers to share ideas with; difficulty in motivating the student as there are no other students for them to bounce energy and ideas off; and students cancel classes last minute more easily (Wisniewska, 2019). Here are some great ways to combat these problems:

1. You can play the role of a student and have your student talk you through what they have learnt. This gives them a chance to practice explaining the concept or idea in their own words.
2. Join online teaching forums and online tutor forums; post questions and experiences in there (be careful to not reveal any student information for safeguarding purposes). You can be a part of a community of teachers that grows and develops together by doing this (Lybarger, 2021).
3. Set up joint sessions/peer tutoring sessions from time to time, where you introduce students that you tutor to each other. This gives them a chance to collaborate and interact with other students. There is a plethora of research that indicates the positives of peer tutoring for both tutee and tutor (Alegre Ansuátegui et al., 2018; Leung, 2019).
4. To help reduce lessons being cancelled, always start and end them with something very fun, like a game or challenge. This keeps positive associations in the student's mind and helps develop an excitement towards beginning a lesson.

There will be more challenges that crop up than the ones that are listed here. The key thing to remember is that there are always ways around these problems. Look to your peers and their experiences; this will often act as a reliable source of information for you to draw from.

A top tip I learnt the hard way is that just because it worked for another teacher does not mean it will work for you. By all means, try out strategies that appear to be logical and will create some success; however, do not expect them to work all of the time. Expect them to maybe work and be prepared for if they do not.

The next section will conclude and recap the main points covered within this chapter.

Conclusion

There are a range of different online class sizes that teachers teach. These are often simplified into three modes of teaching online: 1-to-1 classes, small classes, or large classes (Lu, 2020). When approaching the teaching of these three class sizes, you should consider what the goals and objectives of the class are. You should also consider the opportunities and challenges you may face when teaching these class sizes. This is because as the class size increases, some things are difficult to maintain, such as personalised feedback and student–instructor interactions (Ehrenberg et al., 2001; McKeachie, 1980; Mulryan-Kyne, 2010). For example, larger classes are typically good for the learning of foundational, fact-based knowledge and smaller classes for developing high- order thinking skills (Taft et al., 2019). That being said, teachers have a range of tools at their disposal to navigate the challenges of each class size, such as using technology (Pishchukhina & Allen, 2021), active learning (Hornsby, 2020), making the most of potential peer tutoring opportunities (Alegre Ansuátegui et al., 2018; Leung, 2019), and providing frequent access to online formative assessment tools that provide immediate automated feedback (Pishchukhina & Allen, 2021).

As an online teacher, through proper planning, careful assessment, and consideration of the key learning points from this chapter, you will be equipped to navigate the problems, challenges, and difficulties that you will inevitably face.

Key takeaways

- *One-to-one and small classes are generally known as a good option for development of high order thinking skills and complex knowledge mastery (Taft et al., 2019).*
- *Large classes are generally known to be effective at delivering foundational, factual knowledge, the kind that requires less personalised teaching (Taft et al., 2019).*
- *Smaller classes typically result in higher levels of student engagement, performance, and opportunity for skill development; larger classes generally reap worse results in these domains (Ehrenberg et al., 2001; McKeachie, 1980; Mulryan-Kyne, 2010).*
- *The challenges of teaching increasing class sizes is often compounded in the online teaching environment (Hornsby, 2020).*
- *Teaching smaller classes and 1-to-1 brings its own set of problems: lack of student opportunity for student–student interactions, excess*

amount of student–instructor interaction, and lack of teacher collaboration (Wisniewska, 2019).
- *Great ways to support larger classes (but still helpful to all class sizes) include:*
  - *Make the most of technologies that support students at scale, e.g. formative assessment quiz sites that give real-time feedback. Increased use of these correlates with increased academic performance (Pishchukhina & Allen, 2021). See Chapter 2 for more details.*
  - *Consider the time zones of the student body and prepare materials/assessments that can be used/taken at suitable times to be inclusive. (Hornsby, 2020).*
  - *Use frequent, routine use of plenary questions and break out rooms during lessons to increase student participation.*
- *Great ways to support smaller classes include:*
  - *Plan extension activities in case the content is completed faster than expected. Ensure these are carefully planned so as to be effective (Seymour-East, 2017).*
  - *Make use of whole class projects like presentations that are split between each student.*
- *Great ways to support 1-to-1 classes include:*
  - *Set up peer tutoring sessions/programs so that students can assist each other and increase their chances for student-to-student interactions. Peer tutoring has been shown to benefit both tutor and tutee (Alegre Ansuátegui et al., 2018; Leung, 2019).*
  - *Join teaching/tutoring groups to keep up to date with new ideas/share your own experiences.*

Bibliography

Alegre Ansuátegui, F. J., Moliner Miravet, L., Lorenzo Valentín, G., & Maroto, A. (2018). Peer tutoring and academic achievement in mathematics: A meta-analysis. *URASIA Journal of Mathematics, Science and Technology Education*, 337–354.

Ehrenberg, R. G., Brewer, D. J., Gamoran, A., & Willms, J. D. (2001). Class size and student achievement. *Psychological Science in the Public Interest*, 1–30.

Hendarwati, E., Nurlaela, L., Bachri, B., & Sa'ida, N. (2021). Collaborative problem based learning integrated with online learning. *International Journal of Emerging Technologies in Learning*, 29–39.

Hornsby, D. (2020). Moving large classes online: Principles for teaching, learning and assessment. In *Pedagogy for higher education large classes*. International Conference on Higher Education Advances.

Leung, K. C. (2019). An updated meta-analysis on the effect of peer tutoring on tutors' achievement. *School Psychology International*, 200–214.

Lu, R. (2020). Industry analysis on online education. *Academic Journal of Business & Management*, 2, 125–132.

Lybarger, D. (2021, August). *Educators' experiences with twitter chats as opportunities for personal and professional learning* [Doctoral dissertation, Wilmington University, USA].

McKeachie, W. (1980). Class size, large classes and multiple sections. *Academe*, 24–27.

Mulryan-Kyne, C. (2010). Teaching large classes at college and university level: and opportunities. *Teaching in Higher Education*, 175–185.

Offenholley, K. H. (2014). Online tutoring research study for remedial algebra. *Community College Journal of Research and Practice*, 842–849.

Pishchukhina, O., & Allen, A. (2021). Supporting learning in large classes: Online formative assessment and automated feedback. In *2021 30th annual conference of the European association for education in electrical and information engineering* (pp. 1–4). EAEEIE.

Seymour-East, B. (2017). 100 Activities for fast finishers [Book Review]. *English Australia Journal*, 76.

Shanahan, T. (1998). *Chapter 6: On the effectiveness and limitations of tutoring in reading. Review of research in education*. European Commission.

Taft, S. H., Kesten, K., & El-Banna, M. M. (2019). One size does not fit all: Toward an evidence-based framework for determining online course enrollment sizes in higher education. *Online Learning*, 188–233.

Wisniewska, I. (2019). *Teaching one-to-one*. Retrieved December 28, 2021, from Cambridge English: www.cambridgeenglish.org/images/525581-teaching-one-to-one-part-1.pdf

Zhang, Y. (2013). Does private tutoring improve students' National College Entrance Exam performance? – A case study from Jinan, China. *Economics of Education Review*, 1–28.

Error correction and feedback online

Error correction and feedback were the pet obsessions of an old academic coordinator I had. He would routinely drill our team on timing, methods, and reason/purpose of the feedback and how we dealt with errors. Up until then, I always thought we just helped students correct all of their errors as soon as we saw them. Little did I know, there is more to it than that!

This chapter gives you an understanding of some of the key types of student errors that occur, some key causes of errors, when and why timing of correcting errors is important, and the different methods of correcting errors we have at our disposal. This chapter leads nicely into Chapter 9 on assessment. It should be noted that errors are a great thing; they are where the learning happens. As Vygotski's Zone of Proximal Development put forward, we need to be pushed to where we need a little support to reap maximal benefits (Zaretskii, 2009).

Aims of the chapter

By the end of this chapter, you will know:

- *What are some of the key types of student errors?*
- *What are some of the causes of errors?*
- *When and why timing of error correction is important.*
- *Methods of error correction.*
- *How to use positive error correction.*
- *What ways can you give feedback?*

DOI: 10.4324/9781003250630-8

Error correction and feedback online

Done right vs. done wrong

The following is the same scenario played out in two different ways. Both are of a 1-to-1 class where the teacher is covering a lesson on the states of matter. During Scenario A, the teacher approaches error correction in one way, repeatedly telling the student they are wrong and telling them the correct answer. In Scenario B, the teacher uses a range of methods of error correction. These two approaches produce very different outcomes and learning environments. These examples are taken from an amalgamation of lessons that I have observed, and yes, some of the mistakes I have made myself! As you read them, think about how you might adopt the approaches from Scenario B and avoid the approaches from Scenario A.

Scenario A

The lesson begins with a short discussion about the stages of the water cycle (to recap the learning from the previous lesson). The teacher asks the student, "What are the stages of the water cycle?" The student answers but mispronounces the word evaporation. The teacher stops them instantly and says, "That is wrong, it is evaporation." The student continues.

The next stage of the lesson is discussing different materials around the house, whether they are solid, liquid, or gas. The student shows the teacher a pencil and tells them it is a liquid, the teacher addresses the error the same way as before, pointing out the error as wrong and telling the student the correct answer. The student looks dejected and starts to slump into their chair (which, as we remember, is a big problem; see Chapter 5 on body language).

An experiment is the next stage; the student is asked to make a prediction about what happens when the teacher heats some water in the kitchen. The student predicts the water will bubble when it gets hot.

Once the experiment is underway, the teacher points out again that the student is wrong, telling them that technically, the water boils and evaporates, becoming steam. The student, although enjoying the experiment, is losing confidence and becomes withdrawn.

Next, the student and teacher need to discuss the findings and record them; however, when the teacher asks the student questions, the student remains quiet, unsure of themselves and unable to answer. The teacher recaps the content and the student listens and fills in the recording sheet.

Error correction and feedback online

The lesson ends with a plenary of questions; out of ten questions, the student attempts three, getting two of them correct and one incorrect, and then does not answer any more. The teacher tells the student they need to improve their ability to attempt questions.

The class is over and the teacher leaves, thinking, "Why are my students so shy and scared of getting things wrong?" The student leaves, thinking, "Why can I never get anything right?"

Scenario B

The lesson begins with the same discussion. The student starts to talk their way through the water cycle and mispronounces the word evaporation. The teacher stops them and says: "Is it evarporasion or evaporation?" The student responds correctly and the teacher says well done.

During the stage of the lesson where the student and teacher discuss things around the house, the student rushes around showing many things. They state that a pencil is a liquid; the teacher says: "Are you sure?" The student self-corrects and the teacher praises them, giving them a star on the reward system. The student laughs with joy and looks very satisfied with herself.

The student then makes their prediction that when water is heated, it bubbles. During the experiment, the teacher heats the water, and asks the student what is happening to it. The student responds: "It is bubbling." The teacher asks, "What else is it doing? What can you see happening?" The student responds: "It is getting hot and it is turning into smoke." The teacher claps and says, "Exactly! So, you were right, it does bubble, and it does more; it gets hot, boils, and turns into steam." The student says, "Yeah, it boils and turns into steam."

The teacher and student discuss what happened for the results sheet. The student fills it in, getting it almost all correct. The teacher questions the use of the word bubbles instead of boils; the student self-corrects and gets some verbal praise from the teacher.

The lesson is ended with a plenary of ten questions. The student attempts all ten; they get eight of them correct, The two incorrect answers are corrected using an image of the water cycle that the student can check to self-assess their answer.

Before leaving, the teacher says, "I loved the way you attempted the questions; remember to say new words a few times and write them down/read

Error correction and feedback online

them when you learn them, so you can remember the pronunciation. Oh, and I was very impressed with how well you can figure out difficult questions by looking at images and seeing experiments happen. You are a wonderful Scientist!"

The teacher leaves with a smile on their face; the student leaves feeling confident and assured of their ability in school.

> *The two scenarios here really reflect how approaching the correcting of errors and simple bits of feedback can impact a learner and learning environment. Although not encompassing of everything that is important about feedback and error correction, they give you a snippet of the importance of dealing with these two aspects of education carefully and effectively.*

Introduction

Error correction and feedback can happen in a variety of ways. Dealing with errors well will reap a multitude of benefits; dealing with them poorly can do the exact opposite (Akhter, 2007). Some ground knowledge about the two are presented in this introduction, and then we will delve into some of the more pragmatic information.

A 2021 study revealed that elementary schools would use platforms such as WhatsApp/WeChat and other instant messaging applications to provide feedback as it was considered to be more flexible, timely, and easy to run (Herwin et al., 2021). We are not going to look at platforms for feedback in this chapter; we already discuss potential platform functions in Chapter 2 and will look into them some more in Chapter 9. However, it is worth being mindful of the ways you might utilise the error correction and feedback methods we will discuss.

Error correction typically happens in response to a mistake that is made (Islam, 2007), either behavioural or academic. Feedback is the method by which a teacher gives the student information about their performance (Ferguson, 2011), both behavioural and academic.

Corder (1967) considered error correction to be beneficial in mainly three ways: informing the teacher of learner progress, evidencing how learning is occurring and what strategies the learner utilises, and providing a fundamental opportunity for students to learn (Corder, 1967).

Naimi (2015) indicated that students can and should self-correct and peer correct. This is because it can encourage collaboration/cooperation, students get to share the knowledge they acquire together, and both learners (the one correcting and the one being corrected) get to grow. The teacher can also gain a deeper understanding of student levels through this process (Naimi, 2015).

Having students actively involved in the error correction process has been shown to reap better results than having them passively involved. In one study, students were better able to remember the capitals of states; this was reflected in the same day, next day, and one week later results (Barbetta & Heward, 1993).

It has been demonstrated that the use of repetition, modelling, and prompting improve at-risk students' ability to increase their ability to read correct words per minute. These results were maintained even when substantial breaks in instruction occurred (Malanga, 2003).

A focus on corrective feedback (formative feedback) typically reaps positive results (Irons & Elkington, 2021); when delivered, it should be supportive, within reasonable time frames, non-evaluative, and specific (Shute, 2008). An easy way to think of this is as constructive feedback. This phenomenon is not one that is restricted to the traditional classroom, it has been demonstrated in the online setting repeatedly (Vinagre & Lera, 2008).

It is worth noting that online systems that identify and correct errors/highlight errors for the teacher have been shown to save teachers time, resources and effort; have another look at Chapter 2 on platforms for more (Schraudner, 2014).

Now that we have covered some of the fundamentals of error correction and feedback, we will look at what kind of errors are likely to occur in your online classes, when and why to correct them, and how to correct them, and then finally look at positive error correction.

What are some of the key types of student errors?

There are multiple ways students can make errors in the online classroom, ranging from incorrect answers, all the way to mispronunciation or even failure to demonstrate how they solved a problem. From consulting teaching professionals, it became clear that a good way to categorise student errors is in the following four areas:

1. High frequency errors. These are errors that happen often and repeatedly. They are generally small and do not cause a huge issue to the learning of the content (such as missing capital letters or spelling of words like surprised).
2. Errors that block meaning. These are errors that distort the meaning of what the student is trying to convey (such as confusion of words, inability to pronounce something, or missing punctuation in some key places).
3. Errors that demonstrate a slight lack of understanding. These are errors that indicate the student is somewhat struggling to understand the concepts (such as showing the correct answer for a math question but showing some incorrect working).
4. Errors that demonstrate a severe lack of understanding. These are errors that demonstrate the student has not understood the concept (such as inability to answer or using totally incorrect terms).

Now that we have some ways to categorise errors, let's look at some of the key causes of errors.

What are some of the causes of errors?

Hanna Touchie identified eight key causes of errors; being mindful of these causes can help teachers remain understanding, empathetic, and prepared in relation to error occurrence and management. They are:

1. Simplification. Students over-simplify and miss the point as a result.
2. Overgeneralisation. Students apply knowledge from other domains that are not relevant.
3. Hypercorrection. Over-focus on an error correction can cause it to be overgeneralised into other domains.
4. Faculty teaching. The teacher provides incorrect learning materials and/or delivers the lesson poorly.
5. Fossilisation. The error has been occurring for so long it is deeply embedded in the student's knowledge.

6 Avoidance. Students find some aspect of the learning difficult and/or they are unsure about it so they simply do not attempt it/avoid it.
7 Inadequate learning. The content has not been absorbed well enough and so the manifestation in answers is lacking.
8 False concepts hypothesised. The students make a hypothesis and it is incorrect.

(Touchie, 1986)

There are different ways to think about, group, and categorise errors and their causes, but this is an appropriate depth to begin thinking about more pragmatic, in-class ways of dealing with errors.

When and why timing of error correction is important

Sometimes errors should be corrected immediately, and sometimes they should be corrected after some time has passed, in a delayed manner. Typically, immediately correcting student errors is done to enhance their accuracy regarding the knowledge or skill. Sometimes, correcting an error will come a little later; an example of this would be when a student is giving a presentation or delivering a speech. Waiting till later is a good way to enhance students' confidence and comfort to undertake projects like these (Touchie, 1986).

Some key points to remember about delayed error correction are:

1 It allows students a chance to notice their error themselves.
2 It allows peers to notice the error and correct it.
3 It allows students to build their confidence and ability to act as a risk taker.

Here are some questions to consider when you are approaching error correction:

1 Is the activity suitable for an immediate correction of error?
    a For instance, a mispronunciation during reading can be corrected immediately; however, interrupting a student's presentation would not be appropriate.

Error correction and feedback online

2   Is the error blocking meaning?
    a   If it is, then the urgency to correct it is higher.
3   Is the error high frequency?
    a   If it is, perhaps the student is more able to self-correct.
4   Does the error indicate low or high levels of misunderstanding/confusion?
    a   If the student has mistaken a simple term, the error can be dealt with quite quickly; if not, perhaps a recap of the learning is necessary.

The answers to these questions might not always be clear; however, treat errors diligently and always do your best to address them all. Worst case scenario, take note of them and deal with the ones you missed at the end of class. Learners have been shown to prefer delayed error correction, so theoretically, your students will be happy with this (Salajegheh & Farahani, 2015).

Now that we know a little bit more about when we should address errors, we can look at some key methods of how should you deal with them. The next section will provide a range of methods to deal with errors in your online class.

Methods of error correction

Among the multitude of ways an error can be corrected, the following suggestions have stood out as most effective to me over the years and are well represented in the literature:

1   Providing a model as a pathway for students to notice their mistake. An example of this is if the student mispronounces a word, the teacher stops the student and says the word; the student then attempts to correct their pronunciation of the word.
2   Visual cues are a great tool in your online class. You can have a coloured piece of card that you hold up when a student has made an error; this gives them a chance to correct each other and/or self-correct.
3   Eliciting feedback from the students is a student-centred way of drawing feedback and error correction from the students. This could be done with a simple "Are you sure?" or "Do we have any other ideas?"
4   Students will from time to time need behaviour correction. This can be down to a variety of reasons, and we looked into this in more detail during Chapter 3. What is important to note is that behaviour correction

is best done through rewarding correct behaviours. See Chapter 3 for more information on this.

(Pawlak, 2013)

Self- and peer correction and assessment are left out intentionally; see Chapter 9 on assessment, specifically the assessment as learning section.

A final point on error correction will now be made; this is in relation to positivity and positive error correction.

How to use positive error correction

Something that has stood out to me over the years is that teachers who approach error correction positively reap more than simply enhanced learning; they get a fuller learning environment, decorated with student smiles, high levels of motivation, and positivity.

Online students, like in-class students, are often unconfident about their abilities. This being the case, you should try to avoid giving feedback in a negative way. An example of this is seen repeatedly in our done right vs. done wrong section at the start of this chapter.

Online teachers need to correct errors in a positive and productive way, offer students frequent opportunities to self-correct, and be sure to point out as many good parts of their work as possible, too.

Student-centred error correction is a fantastic option that you can take advantage of. Having students self-correct reduces the chances of students feeling as though they are not good enough (Ramdass & Zimmerman, 2008).

Ensuring that error correction is done in a positive way is of key importance. Students can easily become demoralised by negative comments, especially in the online classroom. Feedback is the way we learn and develop; good feedback is essential for students to reach their potential. Students also need to feel as though the environment is safe and a place where they can engage in dialogue (Fisher & Lipson, 1986)

Some great ways to keep feedback positive are:

- Use positive language.
- Avoid saying things like: "You're wrong."
- Provide constructive feedback (a pathway to improvement).
- Give students the chance a chance to correct themselves.

- When a student corrects their error, praise them and acknowledge this accomplishment.

Although feedback will be covered to some degree in Chapter 9, we are now going to look at some key points regarding feeding back to your students.

What ways can you give feedback?

Feedback is a hot topic in both education and training. In this section, you are encouraged to utilise corrective feedback as research indicates it reaps positive results (Irons & Elkington, 2021). Corrective here means formative – in place to help the formation of students' knowledge and or skills. As mentioned in our introduction, your feedback should be supportive, within reasonable time frames, non-evaluative, and specific (Shute, 2008). A good way to think of how feedback can be delivered is the following three methods:

1. Visual feedback. This is where the online teacher provides a visual cue to show a student how they are doing, such as thumbs up, nodding or shaking your head slightly, or holding up a hand to indicate the student needs to stop and reconsider.
2. Verbal feedback. This is where the online teacher provides spoken feedback, such as "Good job on _____" or "I liked this part, this part could be better, overall good work."
3. Written feedback. This is where the online teacher reviews a student's work and writes down what was good and what could be improved, such as "Nice use of adjectives, try to use more comparisons, great work overall" or "Great use of _____!" When marking work, think about development points for students; write them down on the work and be as positive as possible.

(Konold et al., 2004)

Throughout all forms of feedback, it is wise to consider using more positive praise than corrective feedback. A well-known way to approach feedback is sandwiching. Sandwiching is a great way to ensure you get a minimum amount of two parts positive to one part constructive. On top of that, it starts and ends positive (Procházka et al., 2020). A simple and very short example of this can be seen in Table 8.1.

Table 8.1 An example of sandwiched feedback

Something positive.	Your introduction demonstrated deep knowledge of the water cycle, wow!
Something to improve on.	Your conclusion did not refer to this knowledge.
Something positive.	Your presentation layout fit the requirements perfectly. Amazing work!

A top tip I learnt the hard way is to pick a couple of methods of feedback and stick to/routinise them. This way the students know what is coming. Feedback can be a stressful process, even for adults. Removing the additional stresses caused by not knowing the process makes for a more comfortable process. Remember, you can take notes of all errors throughout the lesson; it is very simple in an online classroom to do that.

Conclusion

Wrapping these ideas together into a conclusion, it is clear that error correction can reap positive rewards or impact negatively, depending on how it is approached (Akhter, 2007). Teachers should provide students with the opportunity to be actively involved in the error correction process as this enhances the outcomes (Barbetta & Heward, 1993); good ways of approaching this include self-correction and peer correction (Naimi, 2015). Overall, when feeding back on an error, a formative approach is best (Irons & Elkington, 2021), one that is non-evaluative and specific (Shute, 2008).

There are a range of reasons that cause errors, ranging from student-centred to teacher-related and even reasons such as "fossilisation," meaning they are occurring as a result of long-term embedding. Errors sometimes require immediate correction and sometimes delayed correction (Touchie, 1986). Approaching when to deal with them can be complicated, but overall, considering the activity and the appropriateness of stopping the students is logical.

Teachers can apply a range of techniques, such as modelling, visual cues, eliciting feedback, and sandwiching to correct errors and give feedback. It is important to know that students need to feel as though the environment is a safe place where they can engage in dialogue (Fisher & Lipson, 1986). Overall, keeping it positive through positive language, constructive feedback, and allowing students to take the lead on their error correction is a good idea.

Key takeaways

- *Errors should be seen as opportunities to grow and learn (Zaretskii, 2009).*
- *Error correction can be both positive and negative, depending on how it is approached (Akhter, 2007).*
- *Technology can be utilised to feed back on errors if needed (Herwin et al., 2021).*
- *Error correction can be beneficial in many ways, such as informing the teacher of learner progress, evidencing learning, and as a growth opportunity for students (Corder, 1967).*
- *Allowing students to be actively involved in the correction process is beneficial (Naimi, 2015); good ways to do this are through self- and peer correction (Barbetta & Heward, 1993).*
- *Focus on giving corrective/formative feedback as opposed to simply pointing out flaws; it should be supportive, timely, non-evaluative, and specific (Shute, 2008).*
- *One way to categorise errors is into the following four groups: high frequency errors, errors that block meaning, errors that demonstrate slight misunderstanding, and errors that demonstrate severe lack of understanding.*
- *These can be caused by a range of factors, such as simplification, overgeneralisation, hypercorrection, faculty teaching, fossilisation, avoidance, inadequate learning, and false concepts hypothesised (Touchie, 1986)*
- *Errors could be dealt with immediately if the activity is one that permits this (such as a reading of quick-fire questions); a delayed approach could be used if the students were making a speech or presentation. There is no perfect way to approach timing – judge it from the context and remember that students tend to prefer delayed approaches (Salajegheh & Farahani, 2015) (not meaning a delayed correction is necessarily better or worse).*
- *Errors can be corrected in your online class using models, visual cues, elicitation of feedback from self/peers, teacher response, repetition, questioning, and many more; it is important to see what works and set up feedback/error correction routines.*

- *Student-centred feedback and correction should be utilised where possible; make sure you prepare the students for this so it does not become a negative process.*
- *Sandwiching feedback by putting the corrective feedback within two positive comments has been shown to reap positive results (Procházka et al., 2020).*
- *Remember, in your online class, you are able to take notes of all mistakes with ease; any missed ones can simply be followed up at the end of class.*

Bibliography

Akhter, T. (2007). *Giving feedback and correcting errors in ESL classroom*. Brac University.

Barbetta, P., & Heward, W. (1993). Effects of active student response during error correction on the acquisition and maintenance of geography facts by elementary students with learning disabilities. *Journal of Behavioral Education*, 217–233.

Corder, S. P. (1967). The significance of learners' errors. *IRAL*, 161–170.

Ferguson, P. (2011). Student perceptions of quality feedback in teacher education. *Assessment & Evaluation in Higher Education*, 51–62.

Fisher, K. M., & Lipson, J. I. (1986). Twenty questions about student errors. *Journal of Research in Science Teaching*, 783–803.

Herwin, H., Hastomo, A., Saptono, B., Ardiansyah, A. R., & Wibowo, S. E. (2021). How elementary school teachers organized online learning during the Covid-19 pandemic? *World Journal on Educational Technology: Current Issues*, 437–449.

Irons, A., & Elkington, S. (2021). *Enhancing learning through formative assessment and feedback*. Routledge.

Islam, M. (2007). *Analysis of error correction done in different schools in Dhaka city*. BRAC University.

Konold, K. E., Miller, S. P., & Konold, K. B. (2004). Using teacher feedback to enhance student learning. *Teaching Exceptional Children*, 64–69.

Malanga, P. (2003). Using repeated readings and error correction to build reading fluency with at risk elementary students. *Journal of Precision Teaching & Celebration*, 19–27.

Naimi, A. (2015). Errors correction in foreign language teaching. *The Online Journal of New Horizons in Education*, 58–68.

Pawlak, M. (2013). *Error correction in the foreign language classroom: Reconsidering the issues*. Springer Science & Business Media.

Procházka, J., Ovcari, M., & Durinik, M. (2020). Sandwich feedback: The empirical evidence of its effectiveness. *Learning and Motivation, 71*, 101649.

Ramdass, D., & Zimmerman, B. J. (2008). Effects of self-correction strategy training on middle school students' self-efficacy, self-evaluation, and mathematics division learning. In *Effects of self-correction strategy training on middle school students' self-efficacy, self-evaluation, and mathematics division learning* (pp. 18–41). *Journal of Advanced Academics*.

Salajegheh, S., & Farahani, A. (2015). Iranian EFL teachers' and learners' perspectives of oral error correction: Does timeline of correction matter? *Latin American Journal of Content & Language Integrated Learning*, 184–211.

Schraudner, M. (2014). The online teacher's assistant: Using automated correction programs to supplement learning and lesson planning. *CELE Journal*, 128–140.

Shute, V. (2008). Focus on formative feedback. *Review of Educational Research, 78*, 153–189.

Touchie, H. Y. (1986). Second language learning errors: Their types, causes, and treatment. *JALT Journal*, 75–80.

Vinagre, M., & Lera, M. (2008). The role of error correction in online exchanges. In F. Zhang & B. Barber (Eds.), *Handbook of research on computer-enhanced language acquisition and learning* (pp. 326–241). IGI Global.

Zaretskii, V. K. (2009). The zone of proximal development: What Vygotsky did not have time to write. *Journal of Russian & East European Psychology*, 70–93.

Assessment – assessing students online

As I finished my Master of Education, I found myself reflecting at the end of module assessments, and how much I learnt from the assessment itself (often, not a lot). I also thought about my weekly tasks and what they brought me (they helped). And I thought about my weekly reflective journals, which required me to reflect on the implementation of learning and how its application is working out (gold dust). Thinking about what your students can take from each assessment is at the heart of this chapter. Reflect on that as you learn about the key concepts and their application.

This chapter covers the main ideas of assessment of, for, and as learning and their application in the online classroom. The chapter will focus on practical ways that teachers can effectively and optimally assess in their online practice. There is also a short note on diagnostic assessments. The conclusion is that assessment needs to be delivered in a way that does not overly stress students or cause them undue anxiety, and that assessment should enhance teaching and learning in a teacher's practice.

Aims of the chapter

By the end of this chapter, you will know:

- *Online assessment's benefits and challenges.*
  - *Overcoming the challenges.*

Assessment – assessing students online

- *What is diagnostic assessment?*
  - *How to use this in your online practice.*
- *What is assessment for learning (AFL)?*
  - *How to use this in your online practice.*
- *What is assessment of learning (AOL)?*
  - *How to use this in your online practice.*
- *What is assessment as learning (AAL)?*
  - *How to use this in your online practice.*

Done right vs. done wrong

The following are two scenarios. One depicts assessment causing trouble, stress, and issues and the other provides an opportunity for teacher and student growth, enhanced teaching and learning, and increased student independence. As you read these two scenarios, think about being the teacher in each one and what might be some ways to move from the more negative scenario to the more positive one. Also, think about what assessment styles you can notice. The students in the class are Grade 2 and they have been learning about the water cycle.

Scenario A

As students appear in the class, to their uninformed surprise, the teacher's screen has "ASSESSMENT LESSON" written in capital letters. Fear, panic, and doubt pour into their minds. The teacher ponders: "I wonder which of these students is able to do the test . . ." The teacher has no idea, as in the weeks prior, no form of assessing of the students' knowledge had been done.

The test is given in the form of a question that the students need to write about to answer. The question is: "Describe what happens in the water cycle." Some of the students start writing immediately, some are clearly searching for things on the computer, and some sit there blankly, looking demoralised.

As some students finish the test, they tell the teacher; the teacher tells them to sit there and wait. Some students ask for help; the teacher tells them no. The atmosphere is dull and dry.

As the lesson draws to an end, the teacher asks the students to take photos of their work and email it over. Most of them manage this, but some end up needing their parents messaging for support: a tedious process for a teacher with 100 students in total.

The class is over and the teacher opens their email. A backlog of messages presents an array of student work, mostly low quality and demonstrating a lack of understanding regarding the topic that has been learnt. Oh well, time to print out all of these papers and mark them.

Feedback to parents goes poorly, too; they are shocked to find their children have been struggling and want to know why they were not informed earlier. I would feel this way, too.

Scenario B

As students arrive, they know it is the end of module test lesson. They are not stressed, though; they feel prepared and have had plenty of opportunities to see how well they are learning the content. The teacher thinks: "Good thing I gave my EAL student David that image support for the key words to help him access this test." The teacher sits calmly, knowing that all of the students who had cracks in their knowledge have had them identified through regular questioning and self-marking mini post-class quizzes.

The students are presented with the question: "State the steps of the water cycle and what happens at each one." They have done questions in this format before and start confidently. One student raises their hand. The teacher goes into a break out room to address the question; the student cannot remember the order very well. The teacher encourages them to try hard and that it is okay if they make a mistake.

Back to class: as some students finish, they review their work to attempt to uplevel their answers. As the lesson comes to an end, the students submit images of their work to a drive link that the teacher has provided. Nice and organised, ready to be marked digitally by adding comment boxes to the images.

One student did not perform as well as the rest of the class; the parents are aware that he needs extra support, though, and are happy to see that some progress has been made. This is easily demonstrated by letting them see his answers from the diagnostic assessment at the start of the module and his weekly quiz scores. Happy students, happy parents, and happy teacher – a productive module has been had.

Assessment – assessing students online

> *The two scenarios depict how assessment can positively and negatively impact students, teachers, and parents. It is important to understand that assessments are more than a simple tool used at the end of a module; they need to be applied frequently throughout the topic. They have uses beyond finding out what students know. They can even act as a fundamental part of a teacher's own learning process.*

Introduction

Assessing students is a process that can be both supportive and destructive. It can boost students up or give them undue stress. When to assess, how to assess, and what to assess will be different based on the purpose of the assessment and the students you are assessing (Reynolds et al., 2010).

We can assess students online using online assessment technologies (e.g. quiz websites); students who perform well in these tend to perform better in traditional examinations, too (e.g. non-online writing tests) (Amoroso, 2005). That being said, it can be more challenging to support students and deliver when there is a large physical distance between student and teacher (Kearns, 2012).

A well-delivered assessment should be related to the content that has been taught (see diagnostic assessments section for exceptions). How to be successful in the assessment should be clearly described and students informed; any rubric should be in student language and designed to be achievable (Tay, 2018). More on this in the upcoming sections on each assessment type.

Assessment data can be collected and used to find out where students are struggling, where they need more support, where the teacher has failed to deliver content effectively, where the course may have been poorly designed and what patterns can be noticed over time (Tay, 2018).

There are a range of ways that we can assess students in the online learning environment. Some common examples/ways to group assessments are written assignments; online discussion; fieldwork; quizzes and exams; and presentations. Each of these brings with it a unique set of benefits and challenges and is more or less relevant at different stages (Kearns, 2012)

A paper relating to data-based decision making indicated that teachers only use assessment-related, data-based decision making in their practice in around 25–50% of their lessons (Kippers et al., 2018). This is an issue that should be considered when teaching, as data-based decision making is an effective approach to improving student learning and achievement (Schildkamp et al., 2012). We will look at how student performance in assessments can be used in more detail as we move through this chapter.

Reflecting on these key ideas, think about your own lessons and how the information here can relate to you and your own context. Next, we are going to look at some key information about online assessments.

Online assessment's benefits and challenges

Before looking at assessment in more depth and detail, there are some key things that will help you understand the fundamentals of assessing students in the online setting. Firstly, utilising programs, applications, and software will make your life easier; this was mentioned somewhat in the previous chapter, but it is now clear that programs like this save an educator's time and resources and help to speed up the identification and assessment of problem areas (Schraudner, 2014).

Computer-based testing was already becoming popular before the Covid-19 pandemic (Hashemi Toroujeni, 2016; Yan Piaw, 2012), and the multiplicity of potential benefits had been considered and elucidated to some degree (Khoshsima & Hashemi Toroujeni, 2017b; Scalise & Gifford, 2006). Some of the key benefits and drawbacks are shown in Table 9.1.

Table 9.1 The benefits and challenges of online assessments

Benefits	Challenges
Teacher grading and feedback time are lessened (Shute & Rahimi, 2017).	Increased risk of plagiarism (Khoshsima & Hashemi Toroujeni, 2017b).
Students' feedback on assessments is given in real time (Bennett, 2001; Bennett, 2003).	Students and staff could have a lack of IT skills (Khoshsima & Hashemi Toroujeni, 2017b).
Assessments can be taken at any time (Khoshsima & Saed, 2014).	Internet issues can block students' access; they may also not have the correct equipment (Bugbee & Brent, 1990).
Technology is now at a standard where this can be done securely and safely (Khoshsima & Hashemi Toroujeni, 2017b).	Different presentations of information due to equipment may hinder or help students taking the assessment (Chapelle & Douglas, 2006).

(Continued)

Assessment – assessing students online

Table 9.1 (Continued)

Benefits	Challenges
Computer-based testing exams produce less stress and anxiety within students (Khoshsima & Hashemi Toroujeni, 2017b).	Additional training may be required for staff; this can be costly with regard to both time and money.
CBT is what most students prefer (Khoshsima & Hashemi Toroujeni, 2017a).	Sometimes, online students are based in different time zones and/or locations, so assessments may fall at awkward times for day for them (Hornsby, 2020).

Overcoming the challenges

Navigating the challenges is of course no simple feat, but it is possible. Some potential ways to combat them include:

1. Increased risk of plagiarism (Khoshsima & Hashemi Toroujeni, 2017b). Deliver tests during lessons and utilise a live video platform while the test is going on; you can even have the students use a screen share mode or point their camera at the task they are completing (provided they are unable to see each other's cameras).
2. Students and staff could have a lack of IT skills (Khoshsima & Hashemi Toroujeni, 2017b). Provide simple guides in student language and demonstration videos.
3. Internet issues can block students' access; they may also not have the correct equipment (Bugbee & Brent, 1990). Record all lessons so students can review if they miss the class; prepare some materials that can be completed if students cannot join due to internet and share them before the lesson.
4. Different presentations of information due to equipment may hinder or help students taking the assessment (Chapelle & Douglas, 2006). Utilise different assessment methods. However, do not change to something completely new every time; better to rotate a few key assessments so students become familiar with them and not overly stressed.
5. Additional training may be required for staff; this can be costly with regard to both time and money. Utilising simple how-to guides and demonstration videos can help if you are working with other teachers that you need to guide.
6. Sometimes, online students are based in different time zones and/or locations, so assessments may fall at awkward times for day for them

(Hornsby, 2020). Utilising different methods of assessment that can be done outside lesson times and on a student's own agenda can reduce this problem (e.g. project-based learning – see Chapter 11 for more information).

Now that we know some of the fundamental knowledge that can support your understanding of assessment, we will look at what diagnostic assessment is and how you can use it in your practice.

What is diagnostic assessment?

Diagnostic assessment is the assessment we do when we want to know what a student already knows. Usually, we use diagnostic assessments at the beginning of a topic, module, unit, or sometimes even before a lesson or task (Sterling, 2005). There are many benefits to the proper usage of diagnostic assessments. These include:

- We have a clearer understanding of what content can be brushed over more quickly and which areas need a bit more focus.
- They allow the teacher to differentiate the lesson to the needs of the students there.
- They are also a useful tool when considering how to group the students in the class – e.g. pairing two students who know nothing about the topic could limit their potential for growth within the lesson, whereas pairing a student who knows nothing with a student who has some knowledge can encourage peer-to-peer learning and help them both grow more.

(Sterling, 2005)

This being said, ensure you deliver these assessments carefully; giving students assessments on topics they know nothing about can cause them to feel overwhelmed and/or stressed (Sterling, 2005). Let's move on to some practical application.

How to use this in your online practice

There are many platforms and applications that you can use to support your diagnostic assessments, e.g. Quizlet, Kahoot, and Plickers; an added benefit of these is that you can collect data using them. Using online platforms to support you in this stage can be helpful (Csapó & Molnár, 2019); however, it can also complicate things, take up extra time, and make this seem like more of a test than it needs to.

Here are three simple low/no prep diagnostic assessments that have been helpful to me over the years:

1. Red Card Green Card. Students need a red piece of card and a green piece of card. You make statements; they hold up green for yes or red for no. If you want to reduce copying, have them close their eyes (this can be done with thumbs up and thumbs down if they can't get card).
2. Break out group talks. Give the students the topic title and ask them to tell each other what they know; you can move between the groups and gauge their current levels.
3. Pre-lesson fact lists. Students make a list of facts relating to the topic that they already know. The risk here is that parents use a search engine with them and they write out a collection of interesting facts that they do not know but are able to copy down.

Try not to overly rely upon any one approach. Online platforms are helpful, as are these three suggestions. One thing to note – right at the start of a module or topic, perhaps consider using a website or app that helps you collect data. Plickers is one I have used that does this, but it does require some preparation (see Chapter 2); again, I am not advocating any one platform or site – there are many more, and it is always wise to speak to colleagues and do a bit of digging yourself.

What is assessment for learning (AFL)?

Assessment for learning is fundamentally the assessments you deliver in order to support the students' learning – hence the name assessment for learning, meaning, assessment done for the learning. Some refer to these as formative assessments. Assessment for learning has been demonstrated to be a great tool for improving academic performance. Essentially, throughout the module, unit, lesson, or even task, the teacher can deliver mini assessments (Gardner, 2012) to find out a number of things. Some key ones are:

1. Are the students keeping up?
2. What has been difficult and needs revisiting?

3 Are the students retaining the learning?
4 Do the students need extra support?

With this information, the teacher is able to provide the correct support, revision, and guidance to enhance the learning and ensure the students in the class are keeping up with each other.
   (Gardner, 2012)

How to use this in your online practice

Again, apps like Plickers, Quizlet, Kahoot, and other such platforms are useful formative assessment tools that help collect data and record it for you. Teachers also often tend to feel positively about them; however, be aware of internet requirements and time management, as they may be impacted (Demirkan et al., 2017). Then you can review the data to see which students are struggling consistently and what patterns are emerging, and you can begin to think about how to address them. Some low/no prep options that have been helpful to me, can be delivered real time, and give you general feedback during lessons are:

1 Live gap-fill. You speak a sentence and miss out a keyword or term and the students write the missing word. Alternatively, you can speak the first half of the sentence and they can write the ending. While it is hard to gather trackable data like this, it is a great way to see if a term that has been discussed has sunk in.
2 Red Card Green Card. This works for diagnostic and formative assessments; see the diagnostic section for a breakdown.
3 CCQs delivered in a plenary. This is where you ask a one-answer question to the class as a whole and they all need to respond; this can make it difficult to see who exactly is making a mistake but can be useful when used repeatedly throughout a lesson.

Next, let's look at assessment of learning.

What is assessment of learning (AOL)?

Assessment of learning is the process of testing what has been learnt so far; some refer to these as summative assessments. These show the teacher what

Assessment – assessing students online

has been learnt, retained, understood, and is demonstrable at the end of a module or topic. Think back to your exams in school, where you more than likely had to do multiple choice and/or written tests. With this information, teachers can see where students needed more support and where the content may have been too hard or even not delivered effectively. If none of the students in your class understood a concept, there is reason to look more deeply at your own teaching of the concept (Harlen, 2007). Outcomes of assessments of learning are a great tool for teachers to reflect, as you use them in your own practice. Be mindful of this; use the findings and results to develop and enhance your own teaching practice (Harlen, 2007).

A final note before looking at how to use these in your own practice – these tests can cause a lot of distress and anxiety for students. To minimise this, give clear instructions and make sure the test is relevant to the materials covered (Harlen, 2007).

Next, let's see how these can be used in your own online teaching practice.

How to use this in your online practice

As with the previous two sections, platforms can be used for this; specifically, Quizlet and Kahoot can deliver multiple choice tests and even open-ended question tests. Students can cheat at these, so it could be worth asking parents to sit in (although parents may help them cheat, too). The main thing here is to communicate to parents that it is okay if their child scores lowly and that you need to know this if they do so that you can support them and provide the things they need before moving on to the next topic. Some other options of doing these include:

1. Project-based learning. Essentially, the students would complete a project that demonstrates their learning over the course of the module. For instance, if they were learning about circuits, they could build their own circuit. See Chapter 11 for more information.
2. Written tests/coursework/homework assignments. These are where the student either writes an answer to an assigned question during an online live session or complete it as homework/coursework and hand in.
3. Presentations. Presentations are a good way for students to demonstrate their learning and also improve some other skills, such as public speaking and structuring information.

The last section before the conclusion is about assessment as learning. Let's find out what it is and how it can be brought into your online teaching practice.

What is assessment as learning (AAL)?

Finally, there is assessment as learning. This is where the assessment itself is a learning process for the students. The students themselves are at the centre of the assessment process. Self- and peer assessments are examples of this. An example of how effective this is has been shown by large-scale meta-analysis that demonstrated self- and peer assessing is more effective than teacher assessing (Double et al., 2020). Some of the other key benefits of this approach include:

1   It can save you time as much of the assessing is done.
2   Students get more out of the process.
3   It establishes a more student-centric feel to your lessons.
4   It gives students a higher sense of autonomy.

Utilising this approach can be a little more difficult in the online setting, as in the traditional classroom, books can quickly and easily be swapped, while online, swapping some writing can be a lengthier process. That being said, there are still ways to take advantage of this useful tool and integrate it into your practice. Let's look at some. A final comment on the increase of autonomy – education is in place for more than simply teaching facts; enhancing their skills and ability to reflect and develop, so they can function and thrive after school, are important, too (Macur, 2020).

How to use this in your online practice

Assessment as learning can be brought into your online teaching practice in a multitude of ways. Some quick and easy examples are:

1   Two stars and one wish. This is where students give three pieces of feedback to each other (works well with things like presentations in online classes).
2   Having the class assess an old cohort's high standard and low standard pieces of work. This can be done as a group, seeing what makes a good piece of work good and where a poor piece of work could be improved.

3   Self-assessing with a rubric. This is where you provide a rubric for students to self-assess their work. If you do this, make sure it is in student-level language and is not too limiting/constricting of their creativity.

Essentially, any way you can get the students involved in the assessment process can be helpful and productive (as long as you keep it positive and do not overemphasise the potentially negative aspects/feelings that can come with assessment).

Conclusion

Understanding that assessment is one of the cornerstones that supports student learning is a key part of the message that has been conveyed throughout this chapter. That being said, it is clear that it needs to be done carefully and with purpose; when delivered poorly, assessments can do more harm than good (Reynolds et al., 2010).

Utilising the online technologies that are available (e.g. quiz websites) should be done when it is possible and fits the topic; this is because it can take the edge off the grading process and provide much-needed data for teacher consideration. Even more than that, these can support student learning and improve their academic outcomes (Amoroso, 2005). Teachers should consider the benefits and challenges of using computer-based testing systems as they can be both positive and negative. That being said, there are ways to overcome the challenges, and these are usually easily implementable in the teacher's online practice.

Teachers should attempt to make the most of the benefits of a multitude of assessment methods and times (Gardner, 2012). For example, a teacher should use a diagnostic assessment to gauge the students' levels at the start of the topic (Csapó & Molnár, 2019). Following diagnostic assessments, the use of regular formative assessments will highlight any students that need further support and/or areas the teacher has failed to deliver the content (Kippers et al., 2018). Finally, the summative assessment can elucidate to a stronger degree areas of the course that students failed to learn and/or were delivered poorly. These kinds of information are key to course and teacher improvement (Harlen, 2007). Beyond those three approaches, a consideration of assessment as learning and its implementation will enhance a teacher's online practice by giving the students a sense of autonomy and a chance to grow reflectively.

There are a multitude of ways to integrate these methods of assessment into your online practice; some guidance has been provided in this chapter and is reiterated in the key takeaways.

Key takeaways

- *Assessing is an important part of the learning process and can be split into four categories: assessment as, for, and of learning and diagnostic assessments.*
- *Diagnostic assessments allow teachers to find out the students' current knowledge on a topic; they should be delivered at the start of a module (Sterling, 2005). An example would be a Kahoot quiz.*
- *Assessment for learning is when assessments are done routinely throughout a topic with the purpose of supporting the learning of students and ensuring they are keeping up with learning the topic (Gardner, 2012). Examples include CCQs and live gap-fills.*
- *Assessment of learning is done to find out what has been learnt, retained, and understood by students at the end of a topic, and what has been missed. This information can be helpful for developing the course and the teacher's own teaching practice (Harlen, 2007). Examples of this are project-based learning, written tests, and presentations.*
- *Assessment as learning is when assessments are a part of the learning process itself; peer and self-assessing would fall under this bracket, both of which have been shown by meta-analysis to be more effective than teacher assessment (Double et al., 2020). Examples of this include two stars and one wish and self-assessing with a rubric.*
- *Some other common ways to assess in the online environment are written assignments; online discussion; fieldwork; quizzes and exams; and presentations (Kearns, 2012).*
- *Supporting the assessment process through the use of online technologies can help students perform better and save teachers a great deal of time (Amoroso, 2005).*

- *Assessments should be related to the content that has been taught and designed to be achievable (Tay, 2018).*
- *Assessment data can be used for teacher development, course development, and the highlighting of students in need (Tay, 2018).*
- *Using online technologies to support assessment can cause many challenges, such as increased risk of plagiarism and lack of IT expertise for students (Khoshsima & Hashemi Toroujeni, 2017b). These can, however, be combated through simple solutions such as delivering tests during lessons, having formative assessments count towards final grade, and providing simple guides for new platforms (in student-level language).*
- *Overall, aiming for a student-centred assessment that is positive and formative in its nature is optimal. Aim to have clear guidelines and instructions for assessments to reduce stress that students may feel.*

Bibliography

Amoroso, D. (2005). Use of online assessment tools to enhance student performance in large classes. *Information Systems Education Journal*, 1–10.

Bennett, R. E. (2001). *How the internet will help large-scale assessment reinvent itself.* Retrieved January 22, 2001, from Education Policy Analysis Archives: https://doi.org/10.14507/epaa.v9n5.2001

Bennett, R. E. (2003). *Online assessment and the comparability of score meaning.* Educational Testing Service.

Bugbee, A. C., & Bernt, F. M. (1990). Testing by computer: Findings in six years of use 1982–1988. *Journal of Research on Computing in Education*, 87–100.

Chapelle, C. A., & Douglas, D. (2006). *Assessing language to computer technology.* Cambridge: Cambridge University Press.

Csapó, B., & Molnár, G. (2019). Online diagnostic assessment in support of personalized teaching and learning: The eDia system. *Frontiers in Psychology, 10*, 1522.

Demirkan, Ö., Gürışık, A., & Akın, Ö. (2017). Teachers' opinions about "plickers" one of the online assessment tools. In I. Koleva & G. Duman (Eds.), *Educational research and practice* (pp. 476–486). Oxford University Press.

Double, K. S., McGrane, J. A., & Hopfenbeck, T. N. (2020). The impact of peer assessment on academic performance: A meta-analysis of control group studies. *Educational Psychology Review*, 481–509.

Gardner, J. (2012). *Assessment and learning*. Sage.

Harlen, W. (2007). *Assessment of learning*. Sage.

Hashemi Toroujeni, S. (2016). *Computer-based language testing versus paper-and-pencil testing: Comparing mode effects of two versions of general English vocabulary test on Chabahar Maritime University ESP students' performance* [Unpublished thesis submitted for the degree of Master of Arts in TEFL, Chabahar Marine and Maritime University].

Hornsby, D. J. (2020). Moving large classes online: Principles for teaching, learning and assessment. In *Pre-conference event at higher education advances (HEAd) conference (virtual)*. Virtual: Pedagogy for Higher Education Large Classes.

Kearns, L. (2012). Student assessment in online learning. *MERLOT Journal of Online Learning and Teaching*, 198–208.

Khoshsima, H., & Hashemi Toroujeni, S. M. (2017a). Comparability of computer-based testing and paper-based testing: Testing mode effect, testing mode order, computer attitudes and testing mode preference. *International Journal of Computer (IJC)*, 80–99.

Khoshsima, H., & Hashemi Toroujeni, S. M. (2017b). Technology in education: Pros and cons of using computer in testing domain. *International Journal of Language Learning and Applied Linguistics World*, 32–49.

Khoshsima, H., & Saed, A. (2014). Gender differences in using JIGSAW technique II and its contribution to reading comprehension. *International Journal of Language Learning and Applied Linguistics World (IJLLALW)*, 194–207.

Kippers, W. B., Wolterinck, C. H., Schildkamp, K., Poortman, C. L., & Visscher, A. J. (2018). Teachers' views on the use of assessment for learning and data-based decision making in classroom practice. *Teaching and Teacher Education*, 199–213.

Macur, G. M. (2020). The purpose of education. *International Journal of Advanced Research*, 983–985.

Reynolds, C. R., Livingston, R. B., Willson, V. L., & Willson, V. (2010). *Measurement and assessment in education*. Pearson Education International.

Scalise, K., & Gifford, B. (2006). Computer-based assessment in e-learning: A framework for constructing "intermediate constraint" questions and tasks for technology platforms. *Journal of Technology, Learning, and Assessment*, 4, 6.

Schildkamp, K., Lai, M. K., & Earl, L. (2012). *Data-based decision making in education: Challenges and opportunities*. Springer Science & Business Media.

Schraudner, M. (2014). The online teacher's assistant: Using automated correction programs to supplement learning and lesson planning. *CELE Journal*, 128–140.

Shute, V. J., & Rahimi, S. (2017). Review of computer-based assessment for learning in elementary and secondary education. *Journal of Computer Assisted Learning*, 1–19.

Sterling, D. R. (2005). Assessing understanding. *Science Scope*, 33–37.

Tay, H. Y. (2018). *Designing quality authentic assessments*. Routledge.

Yan Piaw, C. (2012). Comparisons between computer-based testing and paper-pencil testing: Testing effect, test scores, testing time and testing motivation. *Computers in Human Behavior*, 1580–1586.

10 Online student welfare and wellbeing

At the core of all educational practice, I have found myself constantly drawn back to the concept of student welfare. While educating students is important, we must do so without having negative impacts on their physical and emotional wellbeing. This chapter is an important one to me and should be to you, too. Please note, I am not a medical professional, doctor, or anything of the sort; while all ideas put forward in this chapter are, to the best of my knowledge, options that can be considered, I am not advocating that you practice them. I am advocating that you review appropriate guidelines for your country and keep up to date with research regarding student welfare in the online lessons. Regarding proper posture and environment setup, see Chapter 5.

This chapter covers ways to ensure students' wellbeing is considered. There are practical techniques provided for eye exercises, moving around, lesson lengths, and safeguarding. The conclusion is that teachers need to be conscious of their students' wellbeing and take measures to protect it.

Aims of the chapter

By the end of this chapter, you will know about:

- *Eye safety during online lessons.*
- *The importance of movement.*
- *Consideration of lesson lengths.*
- *Safeguarding.*

Online student welfare and wellbeing

Done right vs. done wrong

The following are two scenarios where one teacher considers lesson length, eye safety, and the importance of movement; in the other scenario, the teacher does not. Seeing how this impacts the wellbeing of students and the progress of the lesson is eye opening. The students are 6 years old and they are taking part in a math subtraction lesson. As you read these examples, think about how you may consider student welfare in your own online teaching practice.

Scenario A

The 90-minute lesson begins, no breaks, lecture style, and it is no surprise that only 50% of the students show up. The rest caused such a fuss with their parents that they were allowed to miss this class.

The teacher soldiers on, preaching facts for the students to memorise and write down. Thirty minutes into the class, misbehaviour is rife and students are restless or half asleep. One has to leave due to a headache, and the teacher is struggling to control the rest, who are slumped in their chairs with terrible posture.

No time is allocated for movement or stretching, no time for resting eyes from screen time, and breaking up or reducing the length of the lesson is not even considered.

The result: learning goals are missed by almost all of the class, the teacher ends up a ball of stress, and the parents remain unsatisfied. Not to mention, the students leave the class bored out of their minds with headaches, backaches, and low morale.

The teacher too, leaves the class, with a headache and a sore back. "I didn't know teaching online would be this bad!" thinks the teacher.

Scenario B

A 45-minute lesson is scheduled (set up as 20 minutes of learning, a 5-minute break in the middle, and then the final 20 minutes of learning). All of the students show up on time and are ready for class.

The teacher welcomes the students and then starts to play a "stand-up sit-down" game with the class to recap what they can remember from the previous lesson. At the end of the game, a movement routine is used to get the students into the correct sitting posture. Now that the class is focused, has expelled some excess energy, and is seated in a healthy manner, they are ready to deepen their knowledge.

As the first 20-minute section comes to an end, the teacher reminds the students that during the 5-minute break they should follow the 20–20–20 rule; since it has been 20 minutes of screen time, they should look at something 20 feet away for at least 20 seconds. The students are also reminded that they can do some eye-rolling, palming, and focus shifting.

As the second part of the lesson starts, students seem in good spirits and ready for some more learning. The teacher plays another game where the students touch their nose or their heads to respond to questions.

The lesson draws to an end; after the plenary, the teacher asks students to follow 20–20–20 guidance after the class and to do a short bout of eye yoga before they have any other classes.

Students leave the class, well informed, without damage to their health, and ready for another class to come.

> *The two scenarios here depict how simple consideration of recommended guidelines can help to reduce the risk of negative outcomes, such as students missing classes, having headaches, and missing learning goals. Now take a second to think about the negative consequences of not considering student safety and safeguarding protocols such as safer recruitment. Keeping students healthy and safe is the essence of this chapter – read it as such.*

Introduction

Student welfare, in this chapter, is focused on four key areas; however, student welfare as a concept can incorporate all aspects of student safety, health, wellbeing, self-efficacy, and protection (Cornish, 2019; Masters, 2004). The purpose of focusing on these four areas in this chapter is to create some achievable and practical first steps to move towards in the short term. In the medium to longer term, you should consider how to develop, research, and integrate a deeper understanding of student welfare.

Parents, teachers, and students alike have demonstrated growing concerns about the negative backlash from the online learning precautions that have taken place due to Covid-19 (Duraku & Hoxha, 2020). This is some indication that things have perhaps not gone as well as had been hoped. The pandemic has also interrupted and impacted students' opportunities for learning globally (Chiu et al., 2021). Another concerning finding from a survey of over 6500 Grade 4 to Grade 12 students in Canada indicated that elementary students who attended class physically (in person) felt they "mattered" more than other sample groupings who did not (Vaillancourt et al., 2021). This can, to some degree, be cleared up through collaboration, interaction, learning as a group, and the setting of agreed guidelines, among others (Palloff & Pratt, 2007).

Alongside this research, there are indications that students do not sit with correct posture, which can lead to a multiplicity of problems (Kelly et al., 2009) (see Chapter 5 for information and solutions). It is also rational to believe that extended use of computer screens and a lack of movement, spread over overly long lesson times, is also causing negative impacts on student welfare.

These things considered, it is now an important time to consider how our teaching and learning in the online setting can be improved, enhanced, and delivered in ways that support student wellbeing and welfare. This chapter will provide you with some tools to address this in your online practice. This, however, is just the starting place: you should keep up to date with the latest research and information on how to enhance wellbeing, student welfare, and student safety in your online classroom regularly.

Eye safety during online lessons

Keeping our students' eyes protected and safe during our online learning sessions is of key importance. This section will look at some key problems and then discuss tools to deal with them.

An extended period of eye exposure to screens leads to a range of problems that teachers and students should be aware of when engaging with online learning. Some of the key ones listed by the American Optometric Association are:

- Eyestrain.
- Headaches.
- Blurred vision.

- Dry eyes.
- Neck and shoulder pain.

(American Optometric Association, n.d.)

Prolonged exposure to screens can also lead to decreased quality of sleep (Patil et al., 2019), which, as seen in Matthew Walker's book *Why We Sleep*, is detrimental to both learning and health (Walker, 2017).

With this information in mind, it is important to figure out how to combat this in your online practice.

One of the tools advocated by the American Optometric Association is the 20–20–20 rule. This rule recommends taking a 20-second break, every 20 minutes, to look at something 20 feet away from where we are seated. (American Optometric Association, n.d.). This is something that can quite easily be brought into your online teaching practice. Simply set a 20-minute timer and ensure students are getting this momentary break from screen time.

Another possible set of solutions is demonstrated by a 2020 study that showed that ocular yoga exercises positively impacted eye fatigue (Gupta & Aparna, 2020). But how do we use this eye yoga practically in an online lesson?

Allocate a few minutes at the start, middle, and/or end of each class,(depending on the length, think about 20-minute periods of concentration) and routinise it into your lessons. Here are three methods of eye yoga you could incorporate:

- Focus shifting. This is where the students focus on something close by and then focus on something far away.
- Eye-rolling. This is where the students look all the way to the left, then slowly turn their eyes up to the ceiling, then round to the right, then straight down, then back to the left again.
- Palming. This is where you warm the palms of your hands, and then gently rest them over your eyes, covering them for a few minutes.

(Watson & Griff, 2020)

Speaking from my own experience, using eye exercises for just 3 minutes after each 20-minute bout of learning helps students stay focused and could be a contributing factor to why I have very rarely had students complain of headaches. Next, let's look at the importance of movement.

The importance of movement

Without going into too much detail on the activities that you can use that include movement (as some can be seen in Chapter 11), this section will inform you of some of the importance of movement in the classroom and some simple ways to bring it into your online lessons.

There is a multitude of extremely low-cost benefits that can be drawn from incorporating movement into classrooms. Some key areas that are positively impacted are:

- Physical health.
- Mental health.
- Learning.
- Executive functioning.
- Memory.
- On-task behaviour.
- Academic performance.

(Savina et al., 2016)

As it is largely cost-free to get students moving during lessons, and this list of benefits is essentially a teacher's dream list of returns from an invested action, it is clear that this is something that should be taken seriously. Two great options for getting students moving are:

- Movement routines such as pre-lesson stretches, lesson warm-ups, or a tidy your desk routine.
- Action-based activities, for instance stand up for yes and sit down for no (see Chapter 11 for more.)

Routines are the big ones here. If you have a pre-class routine where students stretch out or move around for a couple of minutes, you ensure that all lessons have a bare minimum of student movement. Linking this with the eye routines in the break and having an activity where students get to move around their room a bit would be closer to ideal, though.

The next thing we will look at is the length of lessons.

Consideration of lesson lengths

The number of hours each student spends in online learning might be beyond your control; however, if you have some impact beyond your classes, there are some things to consider.

Dr Poole-Boykin (a child psychiatry fellow at Yale) puts forward a couple of thoughts with regard to the creation of a schedule for learning with children. These are:

1. Students can focus for their age multiplied by between 2 and 5 minutes. For example, if the student is 5 years old, they could focus for between 10 and 25 minutes.
2. Elementary-age students can handle around 1 or 2 hours of instruction per day.

(Poole-Boykin, 2020)

These ideas are echoed in an article by Hannah Hudson that demonstrates the National Board for Professional Teaching Standards in the US agreeing with this idea (Hudson, 2020).

The Office for Standards in Education (OFSTED) in the UK also backs this up through the findings of advice advocating that lessons should be shortened to support student concentration span and reduce screen time (OFSTED, 2021).

Stemming from these ideas, you can create your own lesson lengths; remember to consider adequate break times for students to refresh, move around, and engage in other outlets. The next section is in relation to safeguarding.

Safeguarding

Safeguarding is a term that encompasses everything under the umbrella of the safety and protection of children. Ensuring the safety and protection of children is of the utmost importance; during remote education, it remains just as essential (Gov.UK, 2021). There is no "right answer" to this; you need to be aware of child protection standards globally, not only in your own context. It is also important to be aware of your own behaviours, ensuring not only children's safety but also avoiding putting yourself in compromising situations

(Stewart & Knott, 2002). For this section, we will look to what the National Society for the Prevention of Cruelty to Children (NSPCC) advises. The NSPCC is the UK's leading child protection charity; they also lead a platform that shares the latest news and legislation on child wellbeing, welfare, and protection. The NSPCC also advises in consideration of a multiplicity of areas with regard to safeguarding. Among the list they provide, some key ones are:

- The recruitment of suitable employees. Ensure the school is following suitable safeguarding policies.
- Platform selection. Do some digging. No platform remains suitable forever, so keeping up to date is essential.
- Consent. Students should not be involved in online learning without their consent.
- Live-stream and recording of lessons. This is something that parents and children need to consent to. It is also important to consider who else could be watching and what you are asking students to do.
- Professional boundaries. Students should not be asked to do anything untoward, and as their teacher, you must remain professional and be cautious of your own behaviour and mannerisms.
- Adult to child ratios. During 1-to-1 class, it is wise to have a parent present.
- Contacting children at home. This is only okay as far as parents are aware of it, and parents are encouraged to be involved in this process.
  - NSPCC state: "School staff should only contact children during normal school hours, or at times agreed by the school leadership team."
- Children's wellbeing. Remembering that we are teachers, not professional psychologists, it is good practice to keep an eye on how the students' wellbeing.
  - Think back to the study mentioned in our introduction, which indicated students who are learning online felt as though they "mattered less." Making an effort to find out how students are coping with everything can make a difference.

(NSPCC Learning, 2021)

There are many other aspects of safeguarding that you can be aware of in the online teaching environment. I personally recommend reviewing the NSPCC website and keeping up to date with the latest research and practice advice. You can find this at: www.nspcc.com.

Online student welfare and wellbeing

Conclusion

Consideration of student welfare is essential. This remains true whether in the traditional physical classroom or within the online teaching environment. The precautions that were taken for Covid-19 have given us a new set of problems that were not as central before, such as eye welfare and/or safeguarding online. There are also issues that have been exacerbated, such as student sitting posture (Kelly et al., 2009).

Considering eye safety during lessons, and following simple guidelines like the 20–20–20 rule and eye yoga, could potentially help protect students from eyestrain, headaches, blurred vision, dry eyes, and neck and shoulder pains (American Optometric Association, n.d.), not to mention potentially benefiting sleep quality (Patil et al., 2019).

Another area that should be considered deeply is the importance of movement – for a range of benefits, both physical and mental (Savina et al., 2016). Simply using action-based activities and embedding movement routines into lessons is a good way to ensure this takes place.

Moving on to the consideration of lesson lengths, there is a range of bodies to seek information and advice from. Dr Poole-Boykin advocates shorter lesson lengths, limiting elementary-age students to around 1 or 2 hours of instruction per day (Poole-Boykin, 2020). OFSTED and the UK Government mirror these thoughts (OFSTED, 2021).

Finally, the safety of students is discussed in this chapter. This includes recommendations from the NSPCC such as safer recruiting, the use of safe platforms, and ensuring professional boundaries are maintained. Beyond this, for a teacher's own practice, it is wise to have parents present during lessons, especially when teaching 1-to-1 (NSPCC Learning, 2021).

These ideas all come together into a set of simple approaches to student welfare in the online teaching environment. That being said, this list is not exclusive and is by no means all that should be considered. Teachers should research the regulations and advice of their own country and even find out about global trends in child protection.

Key takeaways

- *Student welfare is of utmost importance, in both a traditional classroom and an online one.*
- *Parents, teachers, and students show concerns about negative backlash from the Covid-19 online learning precautions (Duraku & Hoxha, 2020).*
- *Online lessons can give students a sense that they do not "matter" as much (Vaillancourt et al., 2021). One potential way to impact this is through collaboration, interaction, learning as a group, and the setting of agreed guidelines (Palloff & Pratt, 2007).*
- *Extended bouts of exposure to screens can cause students: eyestrain, headaches, blurred vision, dry eyes, neck and shoulder pain (American Optometric Association, n.d.), and decreased quality of sleep (Patil et al., 2019).*
  - *One potential solution is the 20–20–20 rule (20 seconds of looking at something 20 feet away every 20 minutes of screen time) (American Optometric Association, n.d.).*
  - *Another is eye yoga (Gupta & Aparna, 2020): teachers can use eye breaks and encourage students to practice focus shifting, eye-rolling, and palming (Watson & Griff, 2020).*
- *Involving movement in lessons is a great way to positively impact a range of areas, including physical and mental health, learning, and on-task behaviour (Savina et al., 2016).*
  - *Two methods of involving this in the online environment are "action-based activities" and "movement routines." See Chapter 11 for examples.*
- *Lessons should not be too long; elementary students can handle around 1–2 hours of instruction per day (Poole-Boykin, 2020).*
- *OFSTED in the UK echoes concerns that lessons should not be too long while students are home learning (OFSTED, 2021).*

- *Another method of considering lesson length is to think about children's period of focus time. Dr Poole-Boykin (a child psychiatry fellow at Yale) puts forward a method of calculating this as the student's age multiplied by between 2 and 5 minutes (Poole-Boykin, 2020).*
- *Safeguarding and child protection are integral aspects of teaching online. You should consider the safety of a range of areas, such as safer recruitment, child-friendly platforms, consent, the recording of lessons, live streaming, professional boundaries, adult to child ratios, contacting children at home, children's wellbeing (NSPCC Learning, 2021), and many more! Please do research this more deeply. One potential resource is: www.nspcc.com.*

Bibliography

American Optometric Association. (n.d.). *Computer vision syndrome.* Retrieved January 1, 2022, from American Optometric Association: www.aoa.org/healthy-eyes/eye-and-vision-conditions/computer-vision-syndrome?sso=y

Chiu, T. K., Lin, T. J., & Lonka, K. (2021). Motivating online learning: The challenges of COVID-19 and beyond. *The Asia-Pacific Education Researcher,* 1–4.

Cornish, C. (2019). Student welfare: Complexity, dilemmas and contradictions. *Research in Post-Compulsory Education,* 173–184.

Duraku, Z. H., & Hoxha, L. (2020). The impact of COVID-19 on education and on the well-being of teachers, parents, and students: Challenges related to remote (online) learning and opportunities for advancing the quality of education. *Faculty of Philosophy,* University of Prishtina, *1,* 1–45.

Gov.UK. (2021, March 10). *Safeguarding and remote education during coronavirus (COVID-19).* United Kingdom Government.

Gupta, K., & Aparna, S. (2020). Effect of yoga ocular exercises on eye fatigue. *International Journal of Yoga,* 76–79.

Hudson, H. (2020, March 31). *Kids (and teachers) don't need to spend 8 hours a day on school work right now.* Retrieved January 1, 2022, from We Are Teachers: www.weareteachers.com/virtual-learning-schedule/#:~:text=lt%20features%20recommendations%20from%20the,school%20students%203%2D4%20hours.

Kelly, G., Dockrell, S., & Galvin, R. (2009). Computer use in school: Its effect on posture and discomfort in schoolchildren. *Work,* 321–328.

Masters, G. N. (2004). Conceptualising and researching student wellbeing. *Australian Council for Educational Research,* 1–6.

NSPCC Learning. (2021, May 5). *Coronavirus: 5 steps to update your safeguarding policies and procedures*. National Society for the Prevention of Cruelty to Children.

OFSTED. (2021). *Remote education research: Research and analysis*. Gov.Uk.

Palloff, R. M., & Pratt, K. (2007). *Building online learning communities: Effective strategies for the virtual classroom*. John Wiley & Sons.

Patil, A., Bhavya, S. C., & Srivastava, S. (2019). Eyeing computer vision syndrome: Awareness, knowledge, and its impact on sleep quality among medical students. *Industrial Psychiatry Journal*, 68–74.

Poole-Boykin, C. (2020, March 25). *Homeschooling during COVID-19: Why all kids may not need eight hours of instruction a day at home*. Retrieved January 1, 2022, from Good Morning America: www.goodmorningamerica.com/family/story/parents-teachers-tips-homeschooling-covid-19-kids-hours-69774140

Savina, E., Garrity, K., Kenny, P., & Doerr, C. (2016). The benefits of movement for youth: A whole child approach. *Contemporary School Psychology*, 282–292.

Stewart, D., & Knott, A. (2002). *Schools, courts and the law: Managing student welfare*. Pearson Education.

Vaillancourt, T., Brittain, H., Krygsman, A., Farrell, A. H., Pepler, D., Landon, S., et al. (2021). In-person versus online learning in relation to students' perceptions of mattering during COVID-19: A brief report. *Journal of Psychoeducational Assessment, 40*(1), 159–169.

Walker, M. (2017). *Why we sleep: Unlocking the power of sleep and dreams*. Simon and Schuster.

Watson, K., & Griff, A. (2020, February 6). *Everything you want to know about eye yoga*. Retrieved January 1, 2022, from Health Line: www.healthline.com/health/eye-health/eye-yoga

Activities – online teaching and learning strategies

When I taught my first ever lesson, it was to seven kindergarten students. I had kind of mish-mashed some very high energy activities one after another, and they loved it. For me, it was the most exhausting 30 minutes of my life. They slowly ramped up their energy levels and became wild; afterwards, they were exhausted. I quickly learnt that I needed to grow my battalion of activity options so that I could move between low and high energy activities (stirrers and settlers), in a way that allowed students to master the content and keep up the learning for a whole school day.

Due to the length of this chapter, it may be useful to summarise the chapter's flow. This chapter will first give you a grounded understanding of activities. After that, there are distinct sections, such as teacher-fronted activities, warm-up activities, and project-based learning. In each section, there is a rundown of what these kinds of activities are, followed by different activity suggestions that are very briefly described. Each of these should be considered in a way that might work in your setting. The purpose of this chapter is not to give detailed breakdowns of exactly how to deliver individual activities. It is to give you an understanding of what kinds of categories there are for activities, and examples of activities within these, that you could adapt for your own setting.

Aims of the chapter

By the end of this chapter, you will:

- *Be aware of a range of different activities you can use and the categories they may fall under.*
- *Have been exposed to: setting context, warm-ups, teacher-fronted activities, student-centred activities, project-based learning, routines, differentiation, blended learning, and reflection and wrap ups.*
- *Have a collection of activity ideas that you can adapt and develop for your own teaching practice.*
- *Have an enhanced understanding of the roles activities can play in your online teaching practice.*

Done right vs. done wrong

The following are two scenarios that depict two teachers, one of whom has a range of activities that engage and challenge the students, while the other follows a straight-forward lecturing style. Both classes are for students aged 5 years old and are 20 minutes long. As you read these, think about what activities you might have used, and what activities you might not have used.

Scenario A

The students arrive. As they do, the teacher is sitting silently waiting for them. There is a slightly dull feeling already as they remember the previous lesson's sluggish, boring nature.

Once the lesson begins, the teacher starts to talk at the students and present a lesson through the medium of lectures; although they are supposed to be listening, slowly, they start to lose focus and get distracted. Misbehaviour

Online teaching and learning strategies

frequency increases and most of the information the teacher is talking about is missed and/or ignored.

Halfway into the lesson, many of the children are getting up out of their chairs, and their parents at home are telling them off and encouraging them to go back to their chairs. The students who are not doing this have drained and sleepy looks on their faces.

In the final stage of the lesson, the students have all disengaged or have had to be taken away from the lesson. The teacher now also drained from the constant management of behaviour and repetition of key points that have not been listened to. The plenary assessment is used and clearly indicates the failure of learning. The class is over and everybody leaves, thinking, "Is this really worth it?"

Scenario B

As students join the class, a video is being screen shared of the teacher reading a children's book; this gets the students seated and paying attention while they wait for the class start time.

Lesson begins and a recap of the previous lesson is delivered using a stand-up and sit-down activity. The students all participate and are engaged, and slowly their energy levels being to rise.

The next activity is a class reading with the microphones all muted. Students need to read along with the teacher based on a piece of writing that is being screen shared. The teacher moves the curser over each word so students know where they are up to. This activity settles them down a bit and sets the context for the lesson.

After this, the students are put into break out rooms in groups of three; they are asked to talk about the topic and try to share some things they know so far. Parents are asked to encourage their students to talk in the break out rooms, and the teacher moves between the rooms to monitor. They are allocated 2 minutes for this as they are still quite young.

After this, the teacher pulls them back into the main classroom. The stand-up sit-down activity is used again as it was successful at the start; students know they need to be sensible if they want this game to continue.

As the end of the lesson comes around, the plenary assessment used demonstrates the students have learnt the key points. Everybody leaves smiling and ready for the next challenge their day presents.

I have seen the above two scenarios repeated multiple times by teachers. The use of some engaging and active activities makes a world of difference. I have even seen teachers go from Scenario A teacher to Scenario B teacher in one lesson – that is all it takes. Some back-up, simple activities to draw the students in is something I would recommend to all.

Introduction

What actually is a lesson? A lesson is a series of activities that link and connect to each other, in a balanced and appropriate manner, for the participants of the lesson. Should a lesson be a series of the most exciting activities one after another? While that may seem wise, it can lead to a collection of behavioural and focus-based problems (Urry, 2018). Think about running a marathon: you do not go at a full sprint the whole way; there needs to be some pacing, such that at some stages you maybe go a bit slower, while at other stages you go a bit faster. It has also emerged that engaging students in appropriate activities/learning tasks is one of the teacher practices that most positively impacts student learning in both traditional classrooms and those that incorporate online learning (Anthony, 2019).

Throughout the Covid-19 epidemic, students of all ages were required to study online – bearing in mind, as student groups are younger that their concentration is generally worse, so simply using rote learning and lecturing becomes less effective. Instead, it is better to use a range of approaches, more student-centric in nature (Tinggui Chen, 2020).

A wide scale review by Zhou et al. (2020) highlighted some key ideas relating to the selection of appropriate online teaching resources. These ideas were:

- Appropriate content.
- Appropriate difficulty.
- Appropriate structure.
- Appropriate media.
- Proper resource organisation.

(Zhou & Li, 2020)

What do these ideas mean? Wrapped up nicely, it means that lessons need engaging and interesting activities that keep the students challenged, entertained, and balanced. The setup of all resources should be appropriate and well organised. All of this needs to be done in consideration of student age and concentration spans.

The following sections start off by giving you some background information about the category reflected in the title. Then, you will be provided examples of simple activities ranging from showing an object and asking a question, to giving the students a four-week project to work on. The activities suggested are based on what I have seen to be successful over the years, both teaching online and training teachers in the online setting. They are also adaptations from the literature, and they are what teachers predominantly put forward in the interviews held during the planning stage of this book.

Not all of the activities will suit you, and you will want to change and develop the ones that stand out as useful. That is not only normal – it is great. You should take them as "idea seeds," seeds to plan ideas for you to develop your own activities and approaches. For that reason, the activities are not broken down into detailed step-by-step "how to" guides. They are mentioned and very briefly explained. From here, you can reflect on how you can implement the activity into your practice. If you are struggling, I recommend going to a teachers' group on social media/blog and asking how teachers are using these activities; as discussed earlier in the book, this is a good stand-in for a professional learning community. I have taken the liberty of giving a few contexts in which the activities mentioned might be used.

Setting context

Setting the context is something you do at the start of a lesson. You are showing the students what they are going to be studying in the lesson. You can do this in many ways, such as with pictures, videos, conversation, and storytelling (Gardiner, 2019).

Without setting the context, students may not have a framework of knowledge to work from (Arbib, 1992). They could also lack the motivation to study, as they are likely to fail to connect with the content.

There are many benefits to setting context. Some key ones are:

- Students will see the learning and lesson as more meaningful. This increases their motivation and pushes them to work a bit harder.

- Students' schemas of knowledge are activated; essentially, the things they already know are brought to the surface of their minds.
- Making learning meaningful increases the chances of it sticking. Random, pointless bits of information are filtered out by our brains. We need to feel as though it is useful to remember it.

(Johnson & Sessions, 2014)

Want to know a bit more? The left hemisphere of your brain is more associated with content and facts. The right hemisphere of your brain is more associated with context, story, and relevance to your life (McGilchrist, 2009). Something that struck me a long time ago is that if you do not set the context, you could say that you are not engaging half of a student's brain. This may be a rather reductive way to think about it but does get the point across well.

We will go on to cover some great ways to set the context in your online practice; remember, always use an image related to the topic.

Image-based context-setting

As the name implies, this is where an image is used to set the context of the lesson. There are multiple ways the image can be used; next, you will see three examples of activities that can be done, and contexts they could work in are provided.

Showing a picture

This is where you have a picture loaded up on the sharing screen or the platform. If you are just using video calls, you can have your camera facing an image you have printed out before the lesson. Using questions is a good way to draw up existing knowledge from the students (Dillon, 2004).

For instance, for a science lesson on habitats, you could use images of animals living in their natural habitats and ask the students why these animals live there.

Jigsaw building a picture

This is a more fun way of setting the context with an image. You can do this on the platform you use or by sticking parts of the image to a wall or board behind you. As you stick up parts of the image, students can try to guess what it is. You can reward them if they can guess the answer quickly and turn it into a game of sorts.

For instance, in a math lesson on division, you could build an image of four people and one pizza, then ask the students how all of the people can have some pizza.

Asking the students to show a picture

Before the lesson, you can ask the students to prepare a picture relating to the topic; they could even draw this if they wanted to. Alternatively, as students are arriving, you can ask them to show/draw an image of something related to the topic.

For instance, for a language lesson on food, you could have students bring in images of food and then tell each other what they can see.

Object-based context-setting

This is where the context is set through the use of an object. This could be realia (real life objects) or virtual realia (virtual representations of the objects) (Smith, 1997). Let's look at three examples of activities that can be done. Contexts they could work in are provided.

Showing an object

Having some objects related to the topic ready to show the students is a very effective way of setting the context in an authentic way. Real life objects (realia) give the students an indication that the learning is concrete and has a place in real life (Sadiq, 2019).

For instance, for a science lesson on tooth health, you can show sets of teeth if you have them; if not, you can show the students candies and ask what they think these do to their teeth.

Asking students to prepare an object

Having students prepare objects is arguably better than preparing them yourself. It makes this part of the lesson more student-centred. If you do choose this approach, you will still need to prepare your own, just in case none of the students remember or are able to do this.

For instance, for a language lesson on fruit, you can prepare some real fruit before the lesson and show the students this. You can ask them questions about other fruits they know.

Video-based context-setting

Video-based context-setting is very much like image-based context-setting. Screen share is pretty much a must for this; however, you could send the video out before the lesson for students to watch themselves (much like flipped learning; see the flipped learning section of this chapter). Here are three examples of activities that can be done. Contexts they could work in are provided.

Making your own video

There are simple free apps where you can chop and change videos yourself. Making a video related to the topic yourself does not take too long and can be great for the kids.

For instance, for a language lesson on fruit, you could make a video of some fruit in a supermarket. Then ask the students: "What fruit can you see?"

Showing a short, real-life video

There are millions of relevant videos you can find on the internet. Using clips from documentaries is a simple, authentic way to set the context for your students (Domine, 2011). Always watch the full clip first to make sure nothing inappropriate falls in.

For a science lesson on life cycles, you could show a chicken lifecycle video from a nature documentary. Then ask the students questions like: "What comes out of the egg?"

Showing a short cartoon clip

Just like real-life videos, there are a range of cartoon clips on the internet. You can find ones that are related to almost any topic. If you can find a related clip from a cartoon they love, that is even better.

For example, for a math lesson on addition, you can find a video from a cartoon where somebody needs to count up a payment and ask the students when they have needed to count things up.

Online teaching and learning strategies

Warm-up activities

Warm-up activities get the students prepared for the lesson. They are a bit beyond setting the context, but you can always integrate the two. While there are many different ways to warm students up for the lesson, it is always a good idea to keep the warm-up related to the topic.

Without warming up, student engagement, interest, and motivation can all suffer (Diril, 2015). Often you need to get the students in the zone. Think about a runner: they set their context by putting on their running outfit; then, they warm up before they start the run.

There are many benefits to this. Some key ones are:

- Students who started the class tired can wake up and become energised.
- Students who are shy can begin to emerge from their shells.
- You can further activate existing knowledge banks.
- You can use this to give students an opportunity to expend excess energy; this helps reduce the frequency of misbehaviours.

(Diril, 2015)

The warm-up is a great ice breaker for new students or to introduce the teacher. Your warm-up can also connect the previous week's work or topic with the current one. The more neuron connections students make, the more likely it is they will retain information.

We will go on to cover some great ways to warm the students up in your lessons and provide some examples, too.

Discussion warm-ups

Discussion warm-ups often need very little preparation or materials; they are also a good way to gauge students' enthusiasm and/or current levels of knowledge. Here are three examples of activities that can be done; contexts they could work in are provided.

Whole class discussion

This is the most convenient way to have a discussion-based warm-up in the online environment. It does, however, mean that many of the students will be passive. Use this approach only for short, snappy warm-ups; plenary is a good approach for this.

For instance, for a science lesson on gravity, you can ask students what objects they think will fall slow and which will fall fast. You could extend this by asking: "Why do you think some things are falling faster?"

Pair discussions

It is wonderful if your platform facilitates this through paired chat boxes. If it does not, you would need to push people out into paired break out rooms. This can be time consuming and hard for you to monitor but does maximise the students' talk time.

For instance, for a history lesson on the medieval era, you can ask the students: "If you lived 800 years ago, what would be different in your lives?"

Group discussions

Putting students into groups to discuss the topic is a nice all-round approach for the online classroom. You can monitor groups fairly easily provided there are not too many of them. This may not work perfectly the first time, but once you have done it once or twice, the students will have it down as a routine.

For instance, for a language lesson on past simple, you can ask the students to list things they have done in the past. Give a model yourself first.

Action-based warm-ups

Action-based warm-ups are a great way to get the students moving around. This, as we have seen repeatedly throughout this book, is a low-cost strategy to reap a range of rewards. Here are three examples of activities that can be done. Contexts they could work in are provided.

Listen and act out

Give some instructions for the students to follow. This both gets the students moving and shows you they are participating/listening. It is a great way to get the students a bit more energised and engaged with the lesson. It can be fun and gets their blood pumping, too.

For a science lesson on food chains, for instance, you can tell the students to act out different animals eating their food.

Online teaching and learning strategies

Move and stop

The students can dance around, jump, or do some actions on the spot. When you say stop, they all need to stop. You can connect this to the topic by asking them a question when they stop. You can make it more fun by giving them a reward if the question is answered correctly.

For instance, for a math lesson on addition, you can play move and stop, asking simple addition questions during the stop moments.

Charades

This is a well-known game where somebody acts something out and other people need to guess what they are acting out. It is engaging and fun for the students but only gets one of them moving at a time. Although, you could group the students and have a few students acting out different things, kind of like a race, and similar to how charades is played in person.

For a language lesson on present continuous, you can have the students play charades, acting out different sports or verbs in general (saying what they are doing as they play).

Game-based warm-ups

Game-based warm-ups can include actions or not; either way, they are fun, engaging, and get students involved in the lesson. Here are three examples; contexts they could work in are provided.

Climb the ladder

You draw a ladder on the platform or board behind you. Then, group the students and put their group names at the bottom of the ladder. You follow this up by asking questions; the group that answers the fastest can climb up one step. Repeat this till one team wins; you can give them a reward to motivate them.

For example, for a math lesson on doubling, you can play climb the ladder and ask questions like: "2 times 2" or "5 times 5."

Anagrams

Jumble the letters of the topic or of a keyword from the lesson. As students arrive, they can try to sort the letters out and spell the word. This is more of an individual task and works well with classes that are already very energetic.

For an English lesson on adjectives, you could use three anagrams for this: big, red, and hungry. Once they have figured them out, you can ask them what we use the words for.

Two truths and a lie

You tell the students two true statements and one false one. They have to guess the false one. This gets them thinking about the topic in an engaging way.

For example, for a language lesson on advanced colours, you tell the students some colours you like and don't like; they have to guess which ones you do not like.

Teacher-fronted approach

Teacher-fronted activities are activities where you are centre stage, leading the learning. An example of this is lecturing. This is a widely criticised approach to teaching kindergarten and primary learners. For good reason, too – younger learners are extremely exploratory and this is a fundamental part of learning for them. However, there are some circumstances when this approach is useful (Garrett & Shortall, 2002).

Some key benefits are:

- It is one of the fastest ways to get the point across to students.
- You can ensure key concepts are not missed or skimmed over.
- You can grade the work to ensure base ideas are grasped by even the lowest students.

Some key drawbacks are:

- Students can be disengaged and bored; this is often a passive way to learn.
- Disengagement usually leads to increased levels of misbehaviour.
- Students retain information better when they figure it out themselves.

Usually, using the teacher-fronted activity approach is appropriate when time is short or there is a lot of content to get in. Another reason to use a teacher-fronted approach is when a clear model or demonstration is needed.

It can also be helpful to support students who need it, like EAL students (Balasubramanian & Shunnaq, 2018).

You should avoid using a teacher-fronted approach when the students have the time to explore ideas and learn independently and in groups as opposed to you feeding them the ideas.

We will go on to cover some key teacher-fronted approaches for online.

Demonstrating and modelling

Demonstrating and modelling are key tools for teachers. These are when you show the students what to do. You could complete the task in front of them on the camera or lead them through a task in a step-by-step manner. Let's look at some examples of using this in your online practice in more detail.

Showing them what to do

This is something you would do before having the students do a task or activity. It is the most time-effective way of making sure the students know what they are supposed to be doing. Once you have demonstrated, you can have some strong students re-demonstrate if you have time.

For an example, for an English gap-fill on adverbs, you can show them some examples of how to do a gap-fill on the board behind you.

Telling them what to do

This is the giving of instructions (see Chapter 5). While it is always more effective to demonstrate, sometimes if the activity is straight-forward, it is faster to simply tell them what to do. Better to stage instructions rather than give them all at once.

For a science prediction task on how sugar affects teeth, for instance, you can tell them simple instructions that give them a pathway to making a prediction about how eating too much sugar makes them feel.

Explaining a finished example

This is where you show them a complete piece of work and explain how you made it/got there. It gives them a target to aim for. It is usually quick but can risk all of the students producing identical work, and thus it can hinder creativity.

For example, for a project-based learning task, you can show them a finished model and explain how you got there. They will usually need some form of instructions for project-based learning (PBL) too.

Lecturing

Lecturing as a style of educating is essentially talking somewhat at the students. Although people who are good at lecturing include the students and make it more like a conversation, they also bring in humour, timing, and a logical structure (Domizio, 2008).

When to do it

This is not typically the best way to educate primary and kindergarten learners. However, there are moments where it is relevant. For example: at the start of a lesson; to go over key ideas or concepts; when you are explaining something complicated; or when you are particularly short on time.

For instance, for a multi-disciplinary learning lesson on how humans work, you could use a lecturing style combined with plenary to drill the names for specific bones in the body. This could be turned into a game to encourage students to take part – for example, by having the students race to see who can say it fastest.

When not to do it

You should avoid the lecturing approach when students have time and competency to deal with the concept themselves and there isn't a need for the teacher to take a front seat to provide additional models or take up additional time by lecturing the students through it using step-by-step instructions.

Running through a simple worksheet in a lecturing style can be boring and even counterproductive. Let the students do it themselves and then self-correct through assessment as learning.

Plenary

Plenary is where one person communicates a question or statement that requires a response from the whole class (Slater, 2017). Let's look at three examples of how this can be done; contexts they could work in are provided.

Online teaching and learning strategies

Teacher asks and whole class responds

This is something that can be done to check students are understanding, paying attention, keeping up, and even just to get a bit of participation from the class as a whole.

For instance, for a science prediction task on how sugar affects teeth, you can ask students questions after they learn the key points about teeth health, such as: "Is sugar good for teeth or bad for teeth?"

Plenary can also be student-centred; this would be where the students take on a teacher role and lead questions to the class. It is a good idea to teach your children to screen share for mini teacher moments.

Student-centred activities

Student-centred activities are activities that have student involvement, leadership, and sometimes even creation at their heart. The teacher takes a back seat and acts more as a facilitator and students themselves lead the activity/lesson (Geven & Attard, 2012). They also help to build independence that is connected with their performance when studying online (Zhou & Li, 2020). When teaching online, there are a range of key benefits and challenges regarding the integration of student-centred activities. Let's look at them.

Some key benefits are:

- Students get to develop their ability to take the lead and solve problems without teacher assistance.
- Students become more involved in the learning process.
- Students become more engaged in the learning process.

Some key challenges are:

- These activities can take longer to get the point across.
- Sometimes, students may feel overwhelmed.
- Organising these in the online classroom is more complex than in a traditional classroom as students are not physically together.
- Younger students, especially kindergarten students, need constant monitoring; you cannot send them into break out rooms and expect them to stay on task.

Student-centred activities are often a good tool at most stages of the lesson; that being said, it depends on your students, the topic you are learning and the activity you want to use (Geven & Attard, 2012).

Typically, if the time is tight, and a lot needs to be talked about/covered, using a student-centred approach may not be optimal and should be avoided.

We will go on to cover some key student-centred activities for the online classroom.

Group discussions

Group discussions encourage students to communicate between themselves instead of turning to the teacher. It has also been found that group work and collaboration increase participation and students' engagement levels (Herrmann, 2013). Group discussions need to work a little differently when teaching in an online context; let's look at two different ways of integrating them into your online practice.

Break out group discussions

The simplest approach when attempting to utilise a group discussion in your online practice is to use a break out room function (not including simply talking to the whole class). This is a function where you move students from the main area of the live chat into their own small groups. In these groups, they can talk about the topic or question you have presented them with.

For a science lesson on the states of matter, for instance, you can set each group a different question to discuss like "What solids can you think of?" and "What liquids can you think of?"

Blog post group discussions

Having a student blog area where the class can post comments, answers, questions, or ideas about a topic is another option for discussion to take place. Though, this is more relevant for the upper primary students and maybe the very tech-savvy lower primary students. Kindergarten students will find this too challenging. However, they could, with parent support, post short spoken videos for each other to watch, as long as this is in line with your school safeguarding and parental consent regulations.

For example, for an English lesson on biographies, the students could be required to post a timeline of their chosen person; then, they can comment on each other's timelines and feed back their thoughts.

Presentations

Presentations can be an effective way for students to demonstrate the information they have learnt so far in a lesson or topic (Billington, 1997). They can also be a good way for students to collaborate and create something together, not to mention the added benefit of improving their presentation skills.

PowerPoint presentations

PPT presentations are more for upper primary students (unless children have support from their parents). Getting children used to doing these is beneficial for a variety of reasons, one being the need for these in secondary school, university, and life after school.

For a geography topic on the seven continents, for instance, seven groups of students can present about each of the continents, sharing what they have learnt so far with the class. A good feedback option is for students in the class to add facts they know after the presentation is done.

Show and tell

This is a classic activity that many will remember from being in school. You can often use this as a context setter, warm-up activity, or, from time to time, anywhere else it fits into your lesson. It is a good way to get students moving around, collecting things, and then speaking in front of their peers. It actually works better in an online setting, as students do not need to bring things into school; they have them around them at home already.

For a language lesson where you are teaching about school things, students can hold up and show different stationery pieces that they have and make a simple sentence about what they have got (I have got a pencil).

Poster presentations

Another good option for presentations in your online lesson is to use posters. These can be created digitally or drawn and designed by students at home. You can even teach the students a lesson, have them prepare the posters as homework, and then present their posters in the lesson again, although, there is no necessity for them to be designed as homework. If you have them design them in lessons, they can point their cameras down at the poster they are making and you can give them live advice. The presentation process of the posters can also double up as an assessment opportunity (Billington, 1997).

For instance, for a history class where the students have been learning about the Egyptians, they could design posters of one artefact from Egypt and then explain what it was used for.

Role plays

Role plays are where students act out a character/role in a given context or setting. These can be adapted to a range of topics and subjects with a little bit of teacher creativity. Here are two potential approaches to the implementation of role plays.

Student-created role plays

The students invent and create a role or character from scratch; this character demonstrates learning about the topic that is being learnt by the class. These can be done in a collaborative manner or individually and presented as a speech or monologue.

For a science lesson on the states of matter, you send students into break out groups and they need to figure out what kinds of roles to make to demonstrate the differences in the states of matter (see below for an example).

Assigned role plays with student line creation

Here, you as the teacher create the roles that the students are to undertake; they create the lines. If the students are very young, you can even provide line templates that they can use, or sentence starters.

For instance, for a science lesson on the states of matter, you send the students into break out rooms. Each student is assigned a character, e.g. the ice character, the water character, and the water vapour character. If needed, the students are given instructions that each character needs to describe itself and how it can move into the other two states of matter.

Project-based learning

PBL is a great way to get the students involved in a creative process of physical and student-centred exploration, demonstration, and consolidation of learning (Kokotsaki et al., 2016). PBL can fit into all subjects and required materials can range from small electrical motors and light circuits to pieces of recycled cardboard and old crayons.

Some key benefits are:

- Students get to be physically involved with a creative process relating to the learning.
- Students usually demonstrate high levels of engagement and involvement with PBL.
- PBL is easily made into a collaborative process.
- A clear outcome is demonstrated during PBL, which can also be used for assessment.

Some key challenges are:

- Often, PBL will require students to gather materials that parents may struggle to buy; a potential solution is to advocate the use of recycled materials like washed yoghurt pots and old boxes.
- Collaborative PBL is more difficult when students are not physically in the same area or space.
- When PBL is used at home, often parents will do much of the creative work, taking the chance away from the students.

(Kokotsaki et al., 2016)

PBL is a good option to use when the project requires simple materials that can be easily collected in the home. It is also useful when the project clearly demonstrates the learning objectives. What has worked well for me is to have students create their projects as homework, and then we discuss and review the homework during class time.

Since PBL can be time costly and require organisation and utilisation of materials, when time frames are tight or a lot of content needs to be reviewed in a short period of time, PBL may not be the best option and should thus be avoided. Also, if students are not used to this approach, overwhelming them with multiple PBL tasks could be detrimental; in this case,

Online teaching and learning strategies

expose them to this method of learning a little more slowly and give them the support they need.

We will now look into collaborative projects, individual projects, and multi-disciplinary/thematic projects.

Collaborative projects

Collaborative projects are essentially PBL where students work together in teams and groups to complete the project they are undertaking. While this is somewhat challenging when teaching in an online setting, it is not impossible. Here are some examples of how this can be achieved:

1 Presentations. Students can work on different aspects of a presentation together, then take turns in their delivery.
2 3D designs. Students can each design and create a section of a design, e.g. if the topic was on the rainforest habitat, one student can create a 3D design of one of the four layers of the forest and then share information about their design and what it shows to the class. Students could plan their designs together and as a group, covering all four layers.
3 Role plays. Creating a role play from scratch, and relating it to a topic (as seen in the role plays section within this chapter), is a great way to get students to demonstrate learning.

There are many other ways to integrate collaborative PBL into your online teaching practice. Simply searching online, speaking to peers, and even getting creative yourself are great other places to start.

Individual projects

Individual projects are much simpler to implement within your online teaching practice (that does not mean scrap collaboration; it just means perhaps start off with individual projects and gradually bring in collaborative ones). The fundamental difference is that students create their projects on their own, rather than in collaboration with peers. The above-mentioned methods of PBL also work with individual projects. Some additional ones that work more easily individually are:

1 Research presentations. With kindergarten age, information cards are a must! Research presentations are simple: the students go and research

Online teaching and learning strategies

information, either based on hand outs or online; this can be done as homework. Then, students come back together and deliver a presentation to the class.
2. Poster creation. Very simple and straight-forward: students bring together their learning so far and create a poster that demonstrates their learning.
3. Flashcard design. Students can, throughout a module or topic, create flashcards for the key words as an ongoing project to create a bank of key vocabulary.

As with collaborative PBL, this approach has many potential areas of application and integration, and these suggestions are just a place to start.

Multi-disciplinary learning/thematic projects

Multi-disciplinary learning (sometimes known as thematic or topic) is when multiple subjects are integrated across the curriculum. This gives students a chance to recap, review, demonstrate, and, by proxy, enhance their learning across the whole body of subjects within the curriculum. A good example of this is STEM, the integration of science, technology, engineering, and mathematics. Some examples of projects that integrate multiple topics are:

1. Creating their own pyramids using pieces of card. This project can integrate learning goals from maths (shape and angle) and history (facts about ancient Egypt).
2. Creating their own ancient Mesopotamian water irrigation system from cups, popsicle sticks, string, and straws (there are limitless sets of instructions for projects like this to be found from a simple Google search). This would be a more classical STEM and history activity.
3. Creating their own landscape in a cardboard box. Students get an old shoe box or something similar; then, they choose one of the habitats that you have been learning about (e.g. arctic) and create the landscape, labelling the animals, land features, and key facts. This would integrate science, art, geography, and language in some contexts.

These three examples vary in their complexity. Students being at home needs to be considered, as do the materials students will need. That being said, the third suggestion is a very simple one, where all they need is some cardboard, scissors, glue, colours, and scraps of paper.

Inquiry-based learning

Inquiry-based learning is the process by which students explore and inquire into a topic or subject in order to answer questions and/or gain a deeper understanding. It is very student-centred and often an effective way to help students develop their ability to find out information themselves. This can be more challenging with kindergarten students when teaching online, but they can be supported through the use of more guided and structured inquiry, which we will learn more about in this section (Adam, 2021).

Some key benefits to inquiry-based learning are:

- Students develop their ability to research and find answers without the teacher simply telling them.
- Students have a chance to take the lead in their own learning.
- Students demonstrate higher levels of interest and engagement when learning through an inquiry-based approach.

Some key challenges associated with inquiry-based learning are:

- When working with younger learners, it can be more challenging to implement when teaching online.
- Inquiry-based learning can take students longer to find the answer/come to the conclusion than other approaches, such as lecturing.
- Keeping students on task when they are not physically in the room with you can be difficult.

(Adam, 2021)

An inquiry-based approach can be effective when you have enough time to do it properly; trying to rush it will often not be as successful. It is also important to think about the students in the class, how old they are, how comfortable they are with this style of learning. Judging this yourself is key; slowly expose your students to this style and then you will be more aware of their ability to contend with it.

Typically, when time is short, an inquiry-based approach is not wise and should be avoided. Another potential barrier is the level of independence of your students/their susceptibility to distraction.

Inquiry is often broken up into four approaches: confirmation inquiry, structured inquiry, guided inquiry, and open inquiry. We will look at these

Online teaching and learning strategies

individually and give you examples of how to use them in your online practice.

Confirmation inquiry

This approach to inquiry is where students are provided with the question, answer, and method to reach the answer. Students then follow the process to confirm whether the answer is true or not (Yang et al., 2020). This approach can support younger students, as it gives them a pathway to success.

For example, for a science lesson on evaporation, students are informed of the process and how it works and are then required to follow a research method to prove it. The students need to half fill a glass of water; they then draw a line on the side of the glass and leave it somewhere it won't get knocked over for a day. They look at it the following day and see that some of the water has disappeared. This is very easy for you to get them to set up during the lesson, and you can discuss results during the next live lesson.

Structured inquiry

Structured inquiry, much like confirmation inquiry, expects that the students are not necessarily given an answer. They are provided with the steps to inquiry from the teacher but are not provided an answer to the question. The steps are clear and students are expected to follow them as such (Adam, 2021).

For instance, in a geography lesson, students are informed that there are seven continents in the world and that they differ in many ways. The students are then required to go and research where they are on the earth and to build their own globes. They could research together in break out rooms; this would be a reasonably good homework task, for students to show and tell as a warm-up in the following online class.

Guided inquiry

Guided inquiry is where students are provided a question and materials to solve the question. However, they are required to think of the process themselves (Adam, 2021). This is more easily integrated with the upper primary ages as they should have more experience with independent research and presentation of knowledge.

For an art lesson on abstract art, the students are given the following question: "What makes abstract art abstract?" They can then go off and research this, and present it in any manner they see fit. Typically, students will use posters and presentations.

Open inquiry

Open inquiry is where students are given free rein to explore a topic, researching and discovering questions themselves. This approach fits into a more flexible curriculum like Montessori (Labbe, 2019). However, it can be a useful tool for you to utilise should you complete a topic and you want to give the students a chance to move away from reviewing and start to explore more aspects of the topic that are self-led by personal interest.

For instance, at the end of a thematic topic on saving the world, you can allow students to read books, watch short clips, and do their own research in a lesson, to answer questions that they come up with themselves that relate to this topic. They can then present their new findings to the class in any format they choose.

Routines

Routines, as discussed throughout this book, are a fundamental cornerstone of a teacher's practice. These remain just as important when teaching online as when teaching in a traditional classroom. A routine is something that the students do regularly and in the same way; the three we will look at are attention grabbers, lesson start routines, and lesson close routines (Colvin & Lazar, 1995). We are not including eye yoga in this section as it is well detailed in Chapter 10.

Some key benefits to be reaped when using routines are:

- They give the students an indication that a certain time is approaching or has come, such as the lesson beginning.
- They are a good way to catch students' attention before explaining a key point.
- They can be used to support a range of areas, including drilling language, behaviour support, learning space set-up, and more.

Online teaching and learning strategies

Some key challenges with routines when teaching online are:

- Some routines that may work in a traditional classroom are less effective online (due to a range of issues, such as camera visibility).
- Students may be limited in their ability to move around their rooms; this should be considered when implementing routines.

(Fink & Siedentop, 1989)

A great time to use routines is at the start of an online class, or at the end of a class, to catch students' attention, with an activity such as a routine spelling practice or routine gap-fill.

Let's look at three ways you can use routines in your online teaching practice.

Attention grabbers

Attention grabbers are used to catch all of the students' attention and get them looking at you/focused on what you are going to say/do. These can also be used for behaviour management and bringing students back onto the task at hand. These can be created by you and your students or you can pick some simple ones, such as:

1, 2, 3, eyes on me

The teacher says: "1, 2, 3, eyes on me," and the students say: "1, 2, eyes on you." This brings the students back into focus on you as the teacher. This works very well as a method of stopping students misbehaving or as a way to get their full attention before delivering some key learning points.

(Clapping and saying) 1, 2, 1, 2, 3

Another great option for an online lesson, possibly even better as it incorporates movement in front of the camera, is to clap and say: "1, 2, 1, 2, 3." Students need to follow suit and do the same. It works well as it gets the students to put things down that they may have picked up; it also gets them moving and speaking and paying attention to the teacher.

Hands on heads!

Put your hands on your head and say: "Hands on heads!" When you do this, all of the students need to follow suit and put their hands on their heads.

Online teaching and learning strategies

Again, it is a good way to get them to put down anything that may be distracting them; it also gets them looking at the teacher and in the zone for listening and learning. A great tip – you can reward and/or use praise on the students who do this faster. This makes it into something like a game and gets the class more invested.

A good way to mix this up, if the students start to get bored of it, is simply to change the part of the face (avoid eyes in case students get excited and poke themselves in the eyes). It is best to keep it to the shoulders or parts of the face so it can be visual and not require students to stand up.

Lesson start routines

Lesson start routines are, simply put, routines that you do at the start of a lesson. These are a good way to get students into the mind-set that the lesson is about to begin and they need to put their learning heads on. These routines are also a good way to get students' learning space in order/their posture correct.

Posture-setting routines

If you look at Chapter 5, on body language, you will see clear information about proper posture when in an online lesson. You will also see that two studies indicated that 0% of students start a lesson with proper posture, and as the lesson progresses, posture worsens.

A posture-setting routine could simply be a set of instructions, like this:

1. Everybody stand up.
2. Sit down nicely.
3. Straight backs.
4. Feet on the floor.
5. Listening ears ready.
6. Well done!

Tidy table routines

Students will routinely have toys, things, and distractions all over their table. Another potential lesson-starting routine is a 30-second count being shared on the screen; you simply tell the students: "Tidy table time! Everybody ready on time gets a reward ☺." This can even be used before the posture-setting routine.

Songs

Songs are another way to start your lesson and are particularly good for the younger years. You can make these up yourself or simply scour YouTube for ones that you like. There are plenty of these online – just make sure you vet them first and ensure they are appropriate for the children and the age you are teaching.

Lesson close routines

Lesson close routines function in a similar way to lesson open routines, except they occur at the end of the lesson. Other than the eye exercises that we looked at in Chapter 10, lesson close routines can include songs, stretches, and/or relate to the content of the lesson.

Plenary

Plenary, as mentioned earlier, is where one person speaks and the class responds. Having a routine where at the end of each lesson, you fire out a plenary of yes or no questions relating to the topic, is a good way to integrate a recap and a lesson close routine. This perhaps saves you some time as you can do both simultaneously. This can also be delivered using mini whiteboards and markers if the students have them.

Student feedback time

An end of lesson review on what the students enjoyed and didn't enjoy is a good routine to establish if you are looking for feedback on how to make lessons more enjoyable. It is also sometimes an indication of what they perhaps found too hard. However, do not assume this; if they say they didn't like a section of the lesson, perhaps dig a little deeper and find out why.

Differentiation

Differentiation is the process by which the teacher makes the learning accessible to all of the learners in the class. There are many different ways to differentiate (Deunk et al., 2018). This section will look at differentiating by task, outcome, scaffolds, and time allowed.

Online teaching and learning strategies

Some key benefits to differentiation are:

- All students in the class have a chance to access the learning and complete the task.
- All of the students are presented with adequate challenges with regard to contending with the content.

Some key challenges for differentiation online are:

- It can be harder to give task-based differentiation activities, though break out rooms can alleviate this.
- Students can feel bad about themselves if they are given an "easier" task.

(Blackburn, 2018)

You can use differentiation when there are students in the class who cannot access the curriculum in the same way as their peers, e.g. students with special educational needs or students with EAL (Macur, 2020).

You can avoid using differentiation when the students in the class do not need it. You can also not use it if the students who might need it can access the learning with a bit of teacher support.

Let's look at what these four terms mean and how you can use them in your online teaching practice.

By task

Differentiation by task is where you change the task for the students who are undertaking it. Research has mixed views as to whether this is a beneficial process to follow (McNamara & Moreton, 2016). If you do choose to use this approach, here are some examples of how it can work in your online practice.

- Different levels of worksheet difficulty. Make a worksheet that is easier for students who may find the activity too hard.
- Different levels of project difficulty. Assign a less difficult project for students who may find the project too hard (e.g. a 3-minute presentation instead of a 5-minute presentation).

By time allowed

Differentiation by time allowed is as simple as the name suggests. You allocate a little bit more time for students who may need it so that they can complete the task they are presented with. This approach can take the edge of stress off for students who perhaps take longer to read and write (McNamara & Moreton, 2016). Two contexts you might use this include:

- During writing tests and exams. Should you have an online writing test, you might have a time limit of 45 minutes, but the students who have demonstrated they may need 55 minutes are allowed an extra 10 minutes so they can get their ideas down/answer all the questions.
- Completing a worksheet. If there are some students who need a bit extra time to complete a worksheet you start in class, you could allow them to finish it after class and submit it to you later that day.

Scaffolds

Scaffolds are additional resources that can be provided for students to be able to access the learning. This means that all students should be able to complete the same task, but some are given additional resources to be able to do so (Ankrum et al., 2014). Some good examples of scaffolds you can use in your online practice are:

- Weekly language guides. If there are EAL students in the class, sending them a list of key words that will be learnt at the start of each week can give them the support they need so they do not feel overwhelmed when these terms are used in class.
- Sentence starters. Adding sentence starters to worksheets that you create or sending out a "sentence starters list" to students can help those who need it when they need to complete pieces of writing. You can also screen share these or chat box message them to students who are struggling.
- Completed examples of work. This can be helpful for getting students started with their work in many contexts. A word of warning – this can often lead to students simply copying the example you provide. Often, it is better to model how to do the activity instead.

By outcome

Differentiation by outcome is where you create activities that allow students to push themselves as hard as they can, with each student producing a different outcome (McNamara & Moreton, 2016). This particular approach also allows you more time to move between each student one by one, keeping them on task and supported.

- PBL as mentioned earlier, is a great way for students to explore a topic and create something that challenges them. You will see that all students in the class produce differing outcomes.
- Story writing is another area where students will produce very different outcomes; some can write pages and pages, while others will struggle with two paragraphs. All can feel challenged, though.

Some other good options are posters, presentations, timeline creation, graphic organisers, mind maps, and more.

Flipped learning

Flipped learning is a method of teaching in which the students learn the basics of a topic independently in their own time, and then in the online session, they apply, analyse, evaluate, and create based on the basics they have covered in their own time (El Miedany, 2019). This can be challenging with younger students but is still achievable. For example, having students learn key words for the week, before the lessons, helps them ahead of the curve and frees up some time that would otherwise be spent teaching word meanings in lessons.

Some key benefits to a flipped learning approach are:

- Students get to make the most of the teacher contact time, getting guidance and feedback with regard to the more advanced parts of learning.
- Students get to develop their ability to learn independently.
- Students get to take part in more creative projects.

Some key challenges are:

- Often, some students will not do the prior learning, making the strategy somewhat moot.

Online teaching and learning strategies

- Sometimes, the basics are challenging for some students, so they need teacher support to learn them.

(Bergmann & Sams, 2014)

When to use a flipped learning approach depends on the topic and your students. Introduce this approach very slowly and carefully. Starting as simply as possible and then slowly increasing the complexity of what needs to be learnt before the lesson.

A flipped learning approach should be avoided if the students are really struggling with the basics of the topic and require a lot of teacher input. If you do use one in this circumstance, start very small, even just having students learn one word before the lesson, or read one paragraph.

Pre-reading

As the subheading suggests, you provide the students with a piece of text that they need to read before they start the lesson. Starting off with just a sentence is fine; this can then be increased to a paragraph, or even full text, depending on how the students cope with this.

For instance, for a history lesson on the Mayans, students could read a sentence that states the time in which the Mayans were alive.

Pre-research

Pre-researching is something that is better reserved for the upper primary years, as it is essentially having them research a topic before you teach it. This gives them a chance to exercise some inquiry and some independent learning. It also allows them to share information with each other when they come to the online lesson.

For example, for a science lesson on gravity, you can ask students to research how things fall on different planets.

Pre-learning of vocabulary

Similar to pre-reading, this is a very easy way to integrate flipped learning into your online teaching practice. It works quite well with kindergarten students as their parents can usually help them learn individual words. Even if they do not learn them, often they at least look at them, so when the lesson starts, the word is not completely new to them.

For a math lesson on addition, for instance, students could learn the words plus and equals.

Blended learning

Blended learning is when part of the course is taught in the online setting and part of the course is taught in a traditional classroom. This gives teachers the chance to make the most of both settings. The split of online and physical class time will partially decide how you approach teaching with blended learning. That being said, it is a good opportunity to do creative hands-on tasks in groups when physically together and use the online sessions for running through content (Hrastinski, 2019).

Some potential benefits to be drawn from blended learning are:

- Increased student engagement in lesson times.
- Better use of teacher time.
- Increased learning opportunities.
- Students have more opportunities to set their own learning pace.

Some potential challenges associated with blended learning are:

- Some students may not have appropriate computer software and set-up.
- Planning for this may be new to you.

(Graham et al., 2005)

Let's look at how blended learning could play a role in your online teaching practice.

LOTS online and HOTS in class

LOTS are low order thinking skills (remembering, understanding, and applying); HOTS are high order thinking skills (analysing, evaluating, and creating) (Hartini et al., 2021). In a blended learning environment, you have an opportunity to cover the LOTS when in the online class and the HOTS when in the physical class. This way you can build and create projects in hands-on time together, as this is the process that is most challenging when restricted only to the online setting (though not impossible – you can use PBL quite well when teaching online; see our PBL section in this chapter).

For example, in an online science lesson on food and nutrition, the class can learn about what minerals, vitamins, and nutrients we find in our foods. In the physical class, an experiment can be done to test this.

Reflection and wrap-up

A reflection and wrap-up stage of a lesson is where the lesson comes to an end and the students recap and review the learning that has taken place so far. This stage should not take up too much time unless necessary. Having a few routine reflection/wrap-up activities is a good idea; that way students know what is coming and how to do it. Also, making them fun is a good idea if you want students to participate. It is also better to end the lesson with something nice and enjoyable, as it will be the last thing from the lesson that the student remembers (Hajrulla & Harizaj, 2017).

Some key benefits are:

- Students get to recap their learning.
- The teacher gets to see that students have struggled to learn the concepts and ideas that have been delivered.
- The lesson can end on a positive note.

Some key challenges are:

- Students may be worn out by the end of a lesson and unwilling to participate.
- Students may copy each other during this stage to avoid looking as though they do not understand.

(Butt, 2008)

Reflection and/or wrap-up are activities that go at the end of a lesson and should be used to see what the students have learnt and to close off the lesson in a positive and organised way.

You can also use a recap midway through a lesson to touch on the themes that have been covered so far, allowing students to continue to make sense of what they have been learning.

Plenary

Plenary has been mentioned a couple of times in this chapter; here, we will see how it can be used to close off a lesson. Some examples are:

1. Red Card Green Card. Here, the students answer questions by holding up a red or green card to be visible on the camera (red being no and green being yes).
2. Touch your head or touch your nose. Played in a similar way to the above game.
3. Stand-up sit-down. Played in a similar way to the above game.

A note here – having students close their eyes for touch your head or touch your nose can reduce cheating and copying. This can also be approached as a game to make it more entertaining.

Website quiz

Using a quiz website is another option for a wrap-up. These are discussed in more detail in Chapter 2. However, here are two options that usually have a data collection and auto-grading function:

1. Multiple choice quizzes.
2. Gap-fill quizzes.

If you do use these, try to ensure students complete them before the lesson is over; this way you have a more accurate representation of what the student has learnt (parents can't help). Also, students may forget to do them after class. Review the data from these and use it to reflect on the students' needs and your own professional development.

Conclusion

Activities are the foundation of an online lesson. As such, teachers need to ensure they have a range of activities that can be applied in their online practice. Selecting activities depends largely on the class, the teacher, and the topic that is being taught. That being said, there is no exact right activity to use at a given time; there are many good options that can be used and applied.

Activities can range from teacher-fronted to student-centred; there is a time and a place for approaching activities in either one of these ways (Garrett & Shortall, 2002). Activities can also be differentiated to meet the needs of all learners in the classroom; this is also something that needs to be considered when planning and delivering lessons (McNamara & Moreton, 2016).

Teachers can apply a flipped learning approach or an inquiry-based approach and bring in a whole range of activities throughout their lessons. Understanding this is a key part of developing an effective online teaching practice.

Utilising great context-setting activities and warm-ups helps gets students' schemas of knowledge alive and their expectations set (Diril, 2015). Getting a good balance between teacher-fronted and student-centred activities allows students independence and support (Garrett & Shortall, 2002). Finally, wrapping a lesson up with engaging and clear wrap-up activities reviews the content for the students and shows the teacher who has potentially fallen behind (Hajrulla & Harizaj, 2017). All of this can be supported and enhanced through the proper use of routines (Colvin & Lazar, 1995).

Key takeaways

- *A lesson is a series of activities, chosen to support student learning without being overly focused on stirring up students, as this can lead to behavioural problems (Urry, 2018).*
- *Appropriate activities/learning tasks is one of the teacher practices that most positively impacts student learning (Anthony, 2019).*
- *Online teaching resources should have appropriate content, difficulty, structure, and media and be properly organised (Zhou & Li, 2020).*
- *Setting the context at the start of a lesson wakes up students' existing schemas of knowledge and prepares them for the lesson. This can be done using pictures, images, videos, etc. (Diril, 2015).*
- *Warm-up activities get students prepared for a lesson; this benefits interest, engagement, and motivation (Diril, 2015) and can be*

Online teaching and learning strategies

done using discussions (whole class or break out rooms), action-based warm-ups, game-based warm-ups, and more. Be aware of students' room set-ups when planning these.
- *Teacher-fronted activities* are activities that the teacher leads; these can get the point across to students quickly but can lead to low levels of engagement (Balasubramanian & Shunnaq, 2018). Some examples that work online are demonstrating, modelling, lecturing, plenary, and more.
- *Student-centred activities* are activities that the students lead and are at the centre of; they can take a bit longer than teacher-fronted activities but tend to increase engagement and independence (Geven & Attard, 2012). Some examples that work online are discussions, presentations, role plays, and project-based learning.
  - *Inquiry-based learning* is a student-centred approach to learning where students inquire and explore a topic; this includes confirmation inquiry, structured inquiry, guided inquiry, and open inquiry (Adam, 2021).
- *Routines* are essential to a functioning online practice. Good times to use them are at the start of lessons, end of lessons, and to catch students' attention (Colvin & Lazar, 1995). Trying to make sure routines are both verbal and visible in the camera is a good idea.
- *Differentiation* is a method of making activities accessible to all learners. This can be approached by task, by time allowed, by using scaffolds, and by creating activities that differ by outcome (McNamara & Moreton, 2016). Online appropriate examples are within the differentiation section.
- *Flipped learning* is where students learn key content before the lesson, so they can deal with activities that require higher order thinking skills with the teacher present (El Miedany, 2019).
- *Blended learning* is when part of the course is taught online and part is taught in person (Hrastinski, 2019).
- *A lesson should end with a wrap-up*, e.g. a quiz or plenary. This can help students recap learning and inform the teacher of who needs extra help to learn the content (Hajrulla & Harizaj, 2017).

Bibliography

Adam, G. M. (2021). A multi-disciplinary and inquiry-based learning activity: The seven continents. *Journal of Inquiry Based Activities*, 69–80.

Ankrum, J. W., Genest, M. T., & Belcastro, E. G. (2014). The power of verbal scaffolding: "Showing" beginning readers how to use reading strategies. *Early Childhood Education Journal*, 39–47.

Anthony, E. (2019). (Blended) learning: How traditional best teaching practices impact blended elementary classrooms. *Journal of Online Learning Research*, 25–48.

Arbib, M. A. (1992). Schema theory. *The Encyclopedia of Artificial Intelligence*, 1427–1443.

Balasubramanian, C., & Shunnaq, S. R. (2018). Teacher-fronted classes. *The TESOL Encyclopedia of English Language Teaching*, 1–13.

Bergmann, J., & Sams, A. (2014). *Flipped learning: Gateway to student engagement*. International Society for Technology in Education.

Billington, H. L. (1997). Poster presentations and peer assessment: Novel forms of evaluation and assessment. *Journal of Biological Education*, 218–220.

Blackburn, B. R. (2018). *Rigor and differentiation in the classroom: Tools and strategies*. Routledge.

Butt, G. (2008). *Lesson planning* (Vol. III, 3rd ed.). Bloomsbury Publishing.

Colvin, G., & Lazar, M. (1995). Establishing classroom routines. In *The Oregon conference monograph* (pp. 203–206). University of Oregon.

Deunk, M. I., Smale-Jacobse, A. E., de Boer, H., Doolaard, S., & Bosker, R. J. (2018). Effective differentiation practices: A systematic review and meta-analysis of studies on the cognitive effects of differentiation practices in primary education. *Educational Research Review*, 31–54.

Dillon, J. T. (2004). *Questioning and teaching: A manual of practice*. Wipf and Stock Publishers.

Diril, A. (2015). The importance of icebreakers and warm-up activities in language teaching. *ACC Journal*, 42–47.

Domine, V. (2011). Building 21st-century teachers: An intentional pedagogy of media literacy education. *Action in Teacher Education*, 194–205.

Domizio, P. (2008). Giving a good lecture. *Diagnostic Histopathology*, 284–288.

El Miedany, Y. (2019). Flipped learning. In Y. El Miedany (Ed.), *Rheumatology teaching* (pp. 285–303). Springer.

Fink, J., & Siedentop, D. (1989). The development of routines, rules, and expectations at the start of the school year. *Journal of Teaching in Physical Education*, 198–212.

Gardiner, L. S. (2019). To make science relevant and relatable, share it in a story. In *AGU Fall meeting abstracts* (pp. ED11A-02). Harvard University Press.

Garrett, P., & Shortall, T. (2002). Learners' evaluations of teacher-fronted and student-centred classroom activities. *Language Teaching Research*, 25–57.

Geven, K., & Attard, A. (2012). Time for student-centred learning? In A. Curaj, P. Scott, L. Vlasceanu, & L. Wilson (Eds.), *European higher education at the crossroads* (pp. 153–172). Springer.

Graham, C. R., Allen, S., & Ure, D. (2005). Benefits and challenges of blended learning environments. In M. Khosrow-Pour (Ed.), *Encyclopedia of information science and technology* (pp. 253–259). IGI Global.

Hajrulla, V., & Harizaj, M. (2017). Six important tips for beginning and ending the lesson. *Philosophy, Social, and Human Disciplines Series*, 41–45.

Hartini, P., Setiadi, H., & Ernawati, E. (2021). Cognitive domain analysis (LOTS and HOTS) assessment instruments made by primary school teachers. *Jurnal Penelitian dan Evaluasi Pendidikan*, 16–24.

Herrmann, K. J. (2013). The impact of cooperative learning on student engagement: Results from an intervention. *Active Learning in Higher Education*, 175–187.

Hrastinski, S. (2019). What do we mean by blended learning? *TechTrends*, 564–569.

Johnson, B., & Sessions, J. (2014). *What schools don't teach: 20 ways to help students excel in school and life*. Routledge.

Kokotsaki, D., Menzies, V., & Wiggins, A. (2016). Project-based learning: A review of the literature. *Improving Schools*, 267–277.

Labbe, D. (2019). *The University of Maine*. Retrieved January 10, 2022, from Labbe, D. (2019). An analysis of the influence a teacher's level of science-based questioning had on the level of science-based questioning of students in a Montessori school.: https://digitalcommons.library.umaine.edu/honors/505

Macur, G. M. (2020). A critical evaluation of an EAL intervention put in place to prepare weaker EAL students for the motivation and language required at the primary stage recommendations for improvement are provided. *International Journal of Advanced Research*, 684–694.

McGilchrist, I. (2009). *The master and his emissary: The divided brain and the making of the western world*. Yale University Press.

McNamara, S., & Moreton, G. (2016). *Understanding differentiation: A teacher's guide*. Routledge.

Sadiq, B. (2019). Attitude of English teachers toward using Realia materials in English foreign language classroom at Baghdad University. *Psychological Science*, 291–412.

Slater, T. (2017). Plenary: The modern professor's teaching toolkit. In *Joint meeting of the Texas section of AAPT, Texas section of APS, and zone 13 of the society of physics students* (pp. 8:25 AM – 9:01 AM). Bulletin of the American Physical Society.

Smith, B. (1997). Virtual realia. *The Internet TESL Journal*, 1–5.

Tinggui Chen, L. P. (2020). Analysis of user satisfaction with online education platforms in China during the COVID-19 pandemic. *Healthcare, 8*, 200.

Urry, A. (2018). Tips for teaching teens: Planning for pitfalls and making it positive. *The ESOL Journal*, 60–66.

Yang, J. M., Sung, Y. T., & Chang, K. E. (2020). Use of meta-analysis to uncover the critical issues of mobile inquiry-based learning. *Journal of Educational Computing Research*, 715–746.

Zhou, L., & Li, F. (2020). A review of the largest online teaching in China for elementary and middle school students during the COVID-19 pandemic. *Best Evidence in China Education*, 549–567.

Things your students should have ready for classes

Something that really made a difference to me, when teaching online, was simple supplies the students could have. Now, obviously, expecting students to have iPads available is, in many circumstances, not appropriate or even realistic. However, there are a range of low-cost materials that you can encourage students to have. If they cannot get them, you can avoid planning lessons using those materials. This will be shown to you in a list form.

There are actually two lists in this section of the book. The second list is the opposite of the first, as it is the things that you do not want students to have available to them.

When looking at the following list, please be aware that having these things available does not mean students should have them on the desk in front of them ready to act as distractions. It simply means, in the room, nicely organised, and ready should they need to be acquired for an activity.

Great things students can have ready for online classes

Among the long list of things that students can bring to class, here are some suggestions to get you started and give you some ideas:

1   Paper. Really useful, you can use this for simple writing activities, spelling games – pretty much anything else you would use paper for in a traditional classroom setting.
2   Card. This comes in handy for project-based learning, where students need to craft things that stand up, like a pyramid in an ancient Egypt module.

3 Calculator. Helpful for a range of reasons, maths and simple calculations being two of them. If students don't bring them, most computers have an app they can use.
4 Dice. These can help if you are having the kids move into break out rooms and play board games. However, there are many online dice apps, too.
5 A soft toy. As long as this is kept far from the desk, so it is not played with, this can be handy during role plays and/or storytelling.
6 Mini whiteboards and markers, A great resource for quick-fire games where students write an answer and show the board to the camera (works well in plenary times).
7 Pre-exposed keyword lists. These are particularly helpful for EAL students in your class; they may also be a part of you introducing a flipped learning approach.
8 Proper posture poster. Make and share a proper posture poster for students to stick up on their walls. This acts as a visual reminder for them (you could do the same with rules posters).
9 All materials that you sent to them. Before lessons, you may need students to print a worksheet. If they are required to do this, having them ready before class saves time for everybody.
10 A sealed water bottle. Having students repeatedly leave to go and get water can be distracting for all. Also, if you do not advise parents to use a sealed water bottle, it is only a matter of time until a student pours a glass of liquid over their equipment.
11 Any software or applications. Have parents download and install any software ahead of lesson time. This way, lesson time is not eaten up. It is also wise out to send a how-to video, especially for the younger students.

There are many other tools that students can have ready for classes; as such, this is a list that you can continue to develop yourself. Now, let's look at some things that you do not necessarily want students to have around them.

Things you do not want students to have around them during online classes

While there are many things that can be used to benefit all in an online lesson, some things do the opposite. Of course, there are circumstances that make things on this list potentially useful. For instance, a soft toy could

Things your students should have ready

really go on both lists; there are times when a soft toy in the room acts as a distraction and times it functions as a role play prop. This is something you need to navigate as the teacher and decide when it is appropriate and helpful to your students and topic. Here are some things that, typically, you do not want around the students:

1. Any dangerous objects. This can include unstable heavy objects on the table that could fall on the student, scissors, glass, and forks or knives.
2. Toys. As a general rule, having toys around the students will act as a distraction for them. Informing parents of learning space guidelines such as these is a good way to start.
3. Pets. While it can be amusing for the class to see a cat wander across a student's camera, it can also become a distraction that throws a lesson off.
4. TVs or unnecessary media devices. Phones, iPads, and a TV playing a cartoon in the background will absolutely distract the students in your class.
5. A busy desk. Having lots of things on the table, in front of the students, will lead to distraction. Any resources required for the lesson should ideally be placed neatly on a table or side, behind the student. As and when needed, they can be called upon.
6. Food. Students eating is another potential whole class distraction; it also doesn't really put them in the learning zone, not to mention dirtying their computer equipment.

How to inform parents of these?

There are many ways to get parents informed about the online lesson expectations and standards that you create. Some of the things from these two lists will stand out to you and feel right for your class. Some will not. You will also have some ideas of your own. Making a short online learning guide is a good way to start. Keep it simple, like a poster; that way parents can stick it up in the learning space and it acts as a visual reminder. A plain example is provided in Table 12.1.

Table 12.1 Example online learning space guidelines

Things students can have available	Things to avoid having available
Paper	Any dangerous objects
Card	Toys
Calculator	Pets
Dice	TVs playing cartoons
A soft toy	Tablets
Mini whiteboards and markers	Phones
Keyword lists	A messy desk
The proper posture poster	Food
All sent materials ready	
A sealed water bottle	
All software ready for use	

13 What to take from this book

This final section, before the final note, is a moment of reflection for the reader, coming back to the key questions prefaced at the start of the book. The reader has a final opportunity to go back through the book and think about how the newly learnt information can be adapted and implemented into their reading practice.

Do this, do that!

The purpose of this book is not to give explicit instructions for you on how to be an online teacher. Nor is it to tell you exactly what way you should teach an online class. The purpose of this book is to provide you with a deeper understanding of what both recent and past research has elucidated with regard to the key areas of importance when teaching online. All of this, integrated with the thoughts and findings of hundreds of teachers, teacher trainers, and myself. Now that you have reached the end of it, I encourage you to go back through and read the key takeaways of each chapter; here is where you will find a lot of the gold that lurks within the chapters. Having digested the research put forward and the practical application suggestions and ideas, you are in an advantageous position to think about how this can all be applied to your own teaching practice.

Now you have read this book, ask yourself these questions again – this time, answer them

1. What opportunities are there for you to enhance your practice through the use of platforms? What variety of ways can these platforms support you? Can you reduce your marking workload? Can you provide a more student-centred learning environment through the use of these technologies?
2. What is classroom management? How can classroom management be utilised in an online setting? Can this be positive? What about engaging the students? What options are there for bringing these two concepts to life?
3. How can body language and instructions support your online lessons? What about posture and a proper learning environment set-up?
4. What role do parents play in online learning? How can they support you? What are they worried about? How can you alleviate this worry?
5. How will you approach the teaching of different class sizes online? What challenges and opportunities will this present?
6. How will you correct students' errors online? How will you feed back to your students? How can students' errors provide feedback to you as a teacher?
7. What about assessment? What types of assessment are there? How can you use these in your online practice? How can assessments inform you about the students, curriculum, and yourself?
8. Student welfare is key in online learning. What are some of the core ways to support student welfare when teaching online? How can you integrate these into your practice? Where can you find out information about safeguarding?
9. What kind of activities can you use when teaching online? How will you adapt them to suit your students and lessons?
10. What should students have ready for class? What do you not want them to have? How will you communicate this to parents?

So . . . what do I take?

At this stage, beyond research and practical application, ideas, tricks, tools, and ways of running your online classes, what you take is up to you. The answers you produce to these questions are the creative application of this simple equation:

Everything you did know

+

Everything you know now

=

The version of you now, enhanced and
equipped with a new online teaching toolkit

However you choose to apply these in the future, your own further research and creative adaptation and implementation, is a journey left only to you. Do me a favour, though: share what you learn. Do not feel intimidated to write, speak, and communicate the things that work well for you. Who knows, maybe one day I will be reading your book, asking myself a set of questions prefaced by you.

Final note

This has been an incredible challenge and journey for me. As it draws to an end, I am reminded of everybody that I need to express my gratitude and thanks to.

To the reader

Thank you for taking the time to read this book. I hope that it has acted as not only a book of informative research but also as a set of practical tools for you to utilise, enhancing your online teaching practice in a way that makes your life easier. I wrote this book embedded with short stories from real-world scenarios; these were purposeful, to give you not only some context (which we all know is essential now!), but also an example of how tools are useful and the way they impact the outcomes within and after a teaching and learning session. They were also in place to create an engaging read, one that you looked forward to picking up. This is the culmination of years of teaching, training, reading, and writing. I wish you all the best in your application and further growth as a teacher.

To the publisher

Thank you for your patience with me as I worked through this project. I also extend my gratitude for the guidance you have provided at each step of this journey. This has been fundamental to developing of this book and ensuring its quality. I look forward to future endeavours together.

Final note

To my mentors

Without you, none of this would have been possible. This is something for everybody to consider, too. At every stage of life, we act both as a mentor and as a mentee. From being in the playground as kids, showing another kid how to play a new game, to starting a new job, to hiring a new staff member, we are always eternally in one of these two places. I express my gratitude to you all so far.

To the people who put up with me disappearing to finish this

To my friends and family, who have put up with my constant obsession over writing this book and talking about the themes within it, you have my gratitude. I know I have had to disappear for long periods of time to get this done, and you have all been there for me. Thanks!

Index

Note: **Boldfaced** page references indicate tables. *Italic* references indicate figures.

1, 2, 3, eyes on me (activity) 168
1-to-1 teaching, overcoming challenges of 98–100

action-based activities/learning strategies 137, 153–154
activities/learning strategies: action-based 137, 153–154; blended learning 175–176; confirmation inquiry 166; context, setting 148–151, 178; differentiation 170–173; flipped learning 173–175, 178; game-based 154–155; guided inquiry 166–167; importance of 177; inquiry-based learning 165–167, 178; open inquiry 167; overview 144, 177–178; pre-learning of vocabulary 174–175; pre-reading activity 174; pre-research 174; projects-based learning 162–164, 173; reflection 176–177; routines 167–170; scenarios, correct vs. incorrect 145–146, *147*; structured inquiry 166; student-centred 158–161, 178; student engagement and 148; Takeaways *178–179*; teacher-fronted 155–158, 178; warm-up 152–155; wrap-up 176–178; *see also specific name*

American Optometric Association 135–136
anagrams (activity) 154–155
Asarbakhsh, M. 14–15, 20
assessment as learning (AAL) 127–128
assessment for learning (AFL) 124–125
assessment of learning (AOL) 125–127
assessment of students: AAL 127–128; AFL 124–125; AOL 125–127; benefits of 121, **122**, 128; challenges of 121–123, **122**; computer-based testing and 121; data 120; defining 120; diagnostic 123–124, 128; importance of 128; methods of, varied 120, 128; overview 117, 128–129; platforms and 125; scenarios, correct vs. incorrect 118–119, *120*; summative 128; Takeaways *129–130*; technology 120, 128; well-delivered/successful 120; *see also* feedback
assigned role plays with student line creation 161
attention grabber routines 168

behavior correction 110–111; *see also* students, misbehavior
blended learning activities/strategies 175–176

Index

blog post group discussions 159–160
body language: benefits of 65; defining 64, 73; importance of 64–65; instructions and, giving 68–71, 73; modelling 71–73, **72**; overview 61, 73; posture 67–68, *69*, 73; for problem solutions 65, **65–66**, *67*; scenarios of using, correct vs. incorrect 62–63, *64*; student engagement and 61; Takeaways *74–75*; task demonstrations 71–73, **72**
Bolliger, D. 53–54
break out group talks/discussions 124, 159
burnout, teacher 27

Cangelosi, J. S. 26
cartoon clip, showing 151
charades (activity) 154
Chen, T. 14–16
clapping (activity) 168
class blogs 85
class reward systems 52
classroom management: benefits of 27–28; concept of, evolving 26; defining 26; greeting students and 35–36; importance of 26; Indonesian study 27; methods of, varied 27; motivating students and 37; operant conditioning and 34–35; overview 23, 37; positive 34–37; proximity praise and 35; relationships and, developing good 35–36; scenarios, correct vs. incorrect 24–26, *26*; student engagement and 36; students' behavior and 28–29, **29–30**; Takeaways *37–38*; teacher burnout and 27; teams and 36; *see also* rules in online classroom
classroom management self-efficacy (CMSE) 27
class size: comparisons of 92; importance of 95; large, overcoming challenges of 96–97, 100; 1-to-1 teams, overcoming challenges of 98–100; overview 92, 99–100; pair chats and 6; range of 92, 99–100; research on 95; scenarios of, correct vs. incorrect 93–94, *95*; small, overcoming challenges of 97–98, 100; Takeaways *100–101*
climb the ladder (activity) 154
collaboration/collaborative projects 48, 163
communication: methods of 85–86, 89; with parents, effective 77, 85–86, 89; *see also* body language; error correction; feedback
completed examples of work 172
computer-based testing *see* assessment of students
concept checking questions (CCQs) 71, 73, 125
confirmation inquiry activity/learning strategy 166
context of activities/learning strategies, setting 148–151, 178
context and meaningful learning 55–57
Corder, S. P. 106–107
corrective feedback 107, 113
coursework assessment 126
Covid-19 2, 147
cues 64–65, **65–66**, *67*, 73, 110, 113; *see also* body language
customer services of platforms 15

David, A. 13
demonstrating tasks 71–73, **72**, 156–157
diagnostic assessment 123–124, 128
differentiation activities/learning strategies 170–173
Di Giulio, R. C. 26
discussion warm-ups 152–153

education, defining 5
English as an additional language (EAL) learners 2

Index

equipment setup for online education 67–68
error correction: benefits of 106–107, 113; causes of student errors and 108–109, 113; defining 106; methods 110–111, 113; modelling and 110, 113; overview 103, 113; in past 103; positive 111–112; scenarios using, correct vs. incorrect 104–106, *106*; Takeaways *114–115*; timing of 109–110; types of student errors and 107–109; visual cues and 110, 113
explaining a finished example 156–157
extrinsic motivation 49–50, 57
eye safety of students 135–136, 140

feedback: benefits of 106–107; corrective 107, 113; defining 106; formative 107, 113; methods 112, **113**, 127; overview 103, 113; in past 103; sandwiching 112–113, **113**; scenarios using, correct vs. incorrect 104–106, *106*; student, eliciting 110, 113; student errors and 107–109; Takeaways *114–115*; verbal 112; visual 112; written 112; *see also* assessment of students
flipped learning activities/strategies 173–175, 178
formative feedback 107, 113

game-based warm-up activities 154–155
gamification 56–57
gestures 64–65, **65–66**, 67, 73; *see also* body language
Glore, P. 13
goals for motivation, future 48
greeting students 35–36
group discussions 153
guided inquiry activity/learning strategy 166–167

hands on heads (activity) 168–169
Henley, M. 26
high order thinking skills (HOTS) 175–176
homework assignments 126
Hrastinski, S. 13
Huang, R. 12
Hudson, Hannah 138

image-based context-setting 149–150
individual projects 163–164
individual reward systems 51
inquiry-based learning activities 165–167, 178
instant message (IM) groups 85
instructional checking questions (ICQs) 71, 73
instructions, giving 68–71, 73
interaction of students *see* student engagement
intrinsic motivation 45–49, 57

Kahoot 16, 20, 125–126
KISS (Keep It Simple for Students) rules 33

large classes, overcoming challenges of teaching 96–97, 100
learner-to-content interactions 54–55
learner-to-instructor interactions 53–54
learner-to-learner interactions 53
learning strategies *see* activities/learning strategies
lecturing 157
lessons: close routines for 170; defining 147; length of 138, 140; start routines for 169
listen and act out (activity) 153
live gap-fill 125
low order thinking skills (LOTS) 175–176

Manning, L. 28
Martin, F. 53–54

Index

McCormack, Gavin 2
meaningful learning and context 55–57
Microsoft forms 87
modelling: body language 71–73, **72**; error correction and 110, 113; teacher-fronted activities/learning strategies and 156–157
motivating students: classroom management and 37; collaboration 48; extrinsic motivation and 49–50, 57; goals, future 48; importance of 47; intrinsic motivation and 45–49, 57; positive reinforcement 47–48; results of, positive 47, 57; reward systems and 37, 50–52
movement routines 137
movement safety of students 137, 140
move and stop (activity) 154
multi-disciplinary learning 164

Naimi, A. 107
National Board for Professional Teaching Standards 138
National Health Service 67
National Society for the Prevention of Cruelty to Children (NSPCC) 139
Nearpod 17, 20
negative rules in online classroom 31–32, **32**
negative student engagement 45
network congestion 14

object: student preparing 150–151; student showing 150
object-based context-setting 150–151
ocular yoga 136
Office for Standards in Education (OFSTED) 138
online, defining 5
online education: access to, increased 2; benefits of 6; Covid-19 and 2, 147; defining 5, 6; equipment setup and 67–68; first experience with 1; groups in, three main 80; growth of 6; information about, basic 5–6; modes of 95; negative outcomes of 2; overview 1, 6; parents and, importance of 77, 80; pedagogy 2, 6; sitting behind computer and, recommendations for 67–68, *69*; structure of book 3–4, 6; student engagement and 41; students' misbehavior and 29, **29–30**; Takeaways 7
online learning: eye safety and 135–136, 140; movement safety and 137, 140; platforms' enhancement of 13, 19; platforms' negative impact on 14–16, 20; platforms and satisfaction with 15–16, 20
online learning guide 184, **185**
online platforms *see* platforms
open inquiry activity/learning strategy 167
operant conditioning 34–35; *see also* motivating students
outcome, differentiation by 173

pair discussion/chats 6, 153
parents: asking for support from 87, 89; avoiding support from 88–89; benefits of involving 82–83, 88–89; Chinese, survey of 81; communication with, effective 77, 85–86, 89; concerns of, global 81–82, 89; importance of in online education 77, 80; Indian, survey of 81; online education and, importance of 77, 80; online learning guide for 184, **185**; overview 88–89; preparation by students, information about 184; problems/barriers to working with, potential 83–85, **84–85**, 89; scenarios, correct vs. incorrect 78–80, *80*; Takeaways of involving 89–90; in UK, survey of 82; in US, survey of 82

Index

pedagogy 2, 6
phone calls to parents 86
picture, showing/building 149–150
platforms: access to 14–15; assessment of students and 125; convenience for teachers and 12–13; customer services of 15; defining 11, 19; design of 14; early 8, 19; enhancement of online learning and 13, 19; function of 11–12; functions to look for in 14–16, 19; negative impact on online learning 14–16, 20; overview 8, 19–20; quality of 16; safe 138–140; satisfaction with online education and 15–16, 20; scenarios of using, correct vs. incorrect 9–11; Takeaways *20–21*; teachers' needs and **18–19**; tools available with *11*; website service 16; *see also specific name*
plenary 125, 157–158, 170, 177
Plickers 17, 19, 125
Poole-Boykin, C. 138, 140
positive classroom management 34–37
positive error correction 111–112
positive reinforcement 47–48
positive rules in online classroom 31–32, **32**
positive student engagement 45
poster presentations 160–161
posture 67–68, 69, 73
posture-setting routines 169
PowerPoint presentations 160
pre-learning of vocabulary activity/learning strategy 174–175
pre-lesson fact lists 124
preparation by students: necessary items 182–183, **185**; parents' information about 184; unnecessary/avoided items 183–184, **185**
pre-reading activity/learning strategy 174
pre-research activity/learning strategy 174

presentations 126, 160–161
project-based learning (PBL) 126, 162–164, 173
proximity praise 35

QR codes 17, 19
Quizlet 16, 20, 125–126
quiz websites 86, 177

Red Card Green Card (activity) 124–125
reflection activities/learning strategies 176–177
register, live 86
relationships, developing good 35–36
resources for teaching, selecting appropriate 147; *see also* activities/learning strategies
reward systems 37, 50–52; class 52; individual 51; motivating students and 37, 50–52; team 33, 51–52
Roca, J. C. 15
role plays 161
routines 137, 167–170
rules in online classroom: importance of 37; instructional 69–71; KISS 33; negative 31–32, **32**; positive 31–32, **32**; setting 31; student-centred 32; teams supporting 33; visual aids supporting 33; *see also* classroom management

safeguarding 138–140
Sandars, J. 14–15, 20
sandwiching feedback 112–113, **113**
scaffolds 172
screen exposure 135–136, 140
self-assessment 128
self-correction 107
sentence starters (activity) 172
shared drive 87
showing students what to do 156
show and tell presentations 160
sitting behind computer, recommendations for 67–68, 69

Index

small classes, overcoming challenges of teaching 97–98, 100
songs 170
story writing 173
structured inquiry learning activity/learning strategy 166
student-centred activities: benefits of 158; challenges of 158; defining 158; group discussion 159–160; presentations 160–161; reasons for using 159, 178; role plays 161
student-centred rules 32
student-created role plays 161
student engagement: activities and 148; benefits of 45–47, 57; body language and 61; classroom management and 36; context and, meaningful learning 55–57; factors in, influencing 45–46; gamification 56–57; importance of 43; interaction patterns 52–55, 57; learner-to-content interactions 54–55; learner-to-instructor 53–54; learner-to-learner 53; learning and 13; negative 45; online education and 41; overview 41, 57; positive 45; research on 43; results and, positive 45; scenarios, correct vs. incorrect 42–43, *43*; Takeaways 57–58; *see also* motivating students
student feedback time 170
students: classroom management and behavior of 28–29, **29–30**; errors of 107–109; eye safety of 135–136, 140; feedback elicited by 110, 113; greeting 35–36; misbehavior of 28–29, **29–30**, 37; movement safety of 137, 140; self-assessment 128; self-correction 107; teamwork and 36; *see also* assessment of students; motivating students; student wellbeing
student wellbeing: concerns about 134–135; defining 134; eye safety 135–136, 140; importance of 132,

140; lesson length and 138, 140; movement safety 137, 140; overview 132, 140; research on 134–135; safeguarding 138–140; scenarios, correct vs. incorrect 133–134, *134*; Takeaways *141–142*
summative assessment 128

Takeaways: activities/learning strategies *178–179*; assessment of students *129–130*; body language *74–75*; classroom management *37–38*; class size *100–101*; error correction *114–115*; feedback *114–115*; function of 4; online education 7; overall/general 186; parental involvement *89–90*; platforms *20–21*; student engagement *57–58*; student wellbeing *141–142*
task demonstrations 71–73, **72**, 156–157
task, differentiation by 171
teacher-fronted activities: benefits of 155; challenges of 155; defining 155; demonstrating and 156–157; lecturing 157; modelling and 156–157; plenary 157–158; reasons for using 155–156, 178
teachers: burnout 27; convenience of platforms and 12–13; greeting students 35–36; platforms and needs of **18–19**; wellbeing 27; *see also* classroom management; teacher-fronted activities
team point/reward systems 33, 51–52
teams and classroom management/supporting rules 33, 36
telling students what to do 156
Tencent 17, 20
thematic projects 164
Thinglink 17, 20
tidy tables routine 169
time allowed, differentiation by 172

Index

tools, classroom/platform 11, *11*
Touchie, Hanna 108
Trowler, V. 44
two stars and one wish feedback 127
two truths and a lie (activity) 155

UNESCO 2

verbal feedback 112
video-based context-setting 151
video calls to parents 86
video, making/showing 151
visual aids supporting rules 33
visual cues 110, 113
visual feedback 112
Vygotski, L. 103

Walker, Matthew 136
warm-up activities: action-based 153–154; discussion 152–153; game-based 154–155
website quiz 86, 177
weekly language guides 172
wellbeing *see* student wellbeing; teachers
whole class discussion 152–153
wrap-up activities 176–178
written feedback 112
written tests 126

Zhou, L. 147
Zone of Proximal Development 103
Zoom 17, 20

Made in the USA
Monee, IL
03 May 2026